Thank you for buying Dead Happy and supporting me in sharing my discoveries and the views of many, to help bring about change for us all, both in our lives and when we die. By purchasing this book, you have played a part in making it available to others.

Lance G Trendall

DEAD HAPPY
Lance G Trendall

LTP

Dead Happy by Lance Trendall

Copyright © 1990 by Lance Trendall who asserts the right to be identified as the author of this work in accordance with the Copyright, Designs and Patents Act 1988.

No part of this manuscript may be copied or published without the permission of the author who can be contacted at the address and telephone numbers below:

ISBN 0 9520472 2 5 Revised and first paperback edition published in 1994 by Lance Trendall Publishing,
PO Box 69, Harpenden, Herts AL5 2LY
Telephone: 0582 461581 Fax: 0582 766488

British Library Cataloguing-in-Print Data. A catalogue record for this book is available from the British Library.

(ISBN 0 9520472 0 9 First Edition comb bound) 1992
by Lance Trendall Publishing

Cover design and typesetting by Allee Trendall
at Smart Design 0582 766322

Part of cover illustration by Nick Baxter
Pendulum illustrations by Dave Martin

In most cases, the names of people in this book have been changed to protect their privacy. Where possible consent has been obtained to quote the experiences of the living and the dead, whose stories are told in this work.

The author does not encourage people to embark on Spirit Communication and discourages people from acting on advice obtained in this way without serious and conscious consideration. The author and publisher accept no responsibility for the actions of those who ignore this advice.

Acknowledgments

All those who have shared their knowledge and experiences with me. Those who have supported me with their friendship even though they find some of my views far from their own. I'm grateful to those people kind enough to have forgiven me in my formative years and those who still do. Allee, my wife, for her loving and tender guidance – without her spiritual development, vision and encouragement this book would have been incomplete. The people who have shared their own Spiritual beliefs and experiences have been invaluable in helping me in my search for a logical truth and I thank them most sincerely, without them this book would never have happened. Alan Sweeney, for his friendship and the suggestion to include testimonials on the cover – this has opened many doors. The Living Game Seminar for being available just when I needed it, to enable me to find the courage to express my beliefs. I truly thank my father for the sacrifice of his life which helped me embark on my search, my mother for her suffering after his death and her strength to continue with my upbringing and education. My brother for his balanced and loving scepticism, which has helped throughout my life to prepare me for other people's opinions and commit to my own.

Contents

1 Foreword 11
2 Most Ghosts Don't Know That They're Dead 15
3 Spirits Show Themselves For Some Good Reason .. 21
4 How To Deal With Ghosts 25
5 My First Haunting 33
6 Ghosts Can Eavesdrop 41
7 Ghostbusting – Rescue Work 45
8 Exorcism 57
9 At Home With Spirit 63
10 Hauntings 67
11 Rescue Work – Problems & Complications 71
12 More Rescue Work – Hauntings 79
13 Rescue Work – Summary 93
14 Ghost Expectations 95
15 Dangers To Watch For 99
16 Why Do We Have Ghosts? 117
17 More On Spirit Communication 121
18 Spiritual Healing 143
19 Pendulum Dowsing 153
20 Pearly Gates 159
21 Question Time 163
22 Two Tough Issues 173
    Children Who Die 173
    The Aborted Foetus 175
23 Afterward 177
    Bibliography & Recommended Reading 180
    Recommended Films & Cassette Tapes 181
    Useful Addresses 182
    Rescue Circle (Opening & Closing) 181
24 Glossary 187

About the author

Lance Trendall was born in England, in 1956 and began to question Religious teaching when his father died eight years later.

Dissatisfied with the lack of logic and frustrated by the apparent contradictions of The Church's teaching, he embarked on his own search for some sensible answers.

After finding that Spiritualism seemed to combine the teachings of Christ with modern information from the 'other side' Lance sought explanations through the mysterious world of psychic phenomena. With over twenty years reading and study behind him along with many years of fixing ghosts and possessed people, this book is the product of his research. This is the book he'd like to have been able to find when he was thirteen and looking for logic and correlation between old and new psychic phenomena.

Hoping that its readers will be able to read his book with temporary suspension of their own faith, prejudice or cynicism, Lance sets out to share his discoveries with the world.

The book offers answers to such questions as: Why do we have ghosts? What is it like being a ghost? What is a poltergeist? Why do some people become ghosts? What is purgatory? What are the "pearly gates"? Is there a Hell? What is Karma? Is there a Devil? What happens when we die?

The book also tells how each one of us can help ghosts to move on and how we can avoid becoming ghosts ourselves.

After success in Estate Agency and property development the author obtained his City and Guilds in bricklaying to 'keep him earthed' and to better understand the metaphor of building on firm foundations. He married and qualified as an Integral Therapist in 1992 and practices marriage, hypnotherapy and hypnohealing. He acts as a marketing and sales consultant and is a salesman for Smart Design – a graphic design company set up by his wife, Allee, who created the book's cover. Lance also gives lectures on ghosts, teaches communication skills and offers consultation on many life issues.

One

FOREWORD

We all like a ghost story, don't we?

From the moment we're born we are curious about everything, yet death and ghosts remain a bit of a mystery right up until we die. As a child, the explanations of the After-life, God, Heaven and Hell were all a bit confusing. I remember wondering how Hell could be compatible with an 'all forgiving' God. Why should we need to go to church to worship – if God is omnipotent surely He could hear me wherever I pray? If God knows everything, surely He'll know why I sinned and through His understanding He would forgive me?

So I began to wonder, what about Hell and Heaven? How could a loving God allow anyone to go to eternal damnation and the fires of Hell?

At school we debated the existence of ghosts, as most adolescents do, ghosts stories were exchanged and experiments with ouija boards, for communicating with the dead, took place in dimly lit rooms.

I had all the usual childhood experiences, but I wanted to find the answers. I wanted to discover a belief or truth that wasn't full of contradictions and inconsistencies. A faith that combined logic and reason with the quest for love and harmony, perhaps even a God. So my search began.

This book is written as a result of that search. I find that whilst there are many great books available, there is not one like this; one that offers a simple and logical explanation for the existence of ghosts, explains what they are like and what it's like to be a ghost.

There are many books on hauntings, I've read more than I can remember, but few explain how to fix the haunting. This book deals with 'ghost therapy', how to help the ghost and why he needs help. Many hauntings have stopped as a result of the methods described in this book and from my work with ghosts.

As well as twenty years experience in dealing with ghosts, my research has included much reading. Many of the books were 'channelled', conceived by a spirit and channelled through a medium, providing a modern insight into our world and the world beyond. Much of that reading has helped to shape my views; as correlation between ancient and modern teaching becomes apparent, it's easier to comprehend both.

The research has included many hours of discussion with people of different faiths. My attendance at regular meetings where spirits and ghosts communicate has been invaluable first hand experience for confirming and fine-tuning the theories expressed here.

The book is designed to fill a gap in our bookshelves by providing many answers and inevitably raising many questions. It is the book I so desperately needed to read myself when I simply was not satisfied with the teaching available on life after death and religion.

I hope that through this book I shall allay fears of ghosts, death, hell and judgment. Through this book I hope to make death so normal that we can reduce the depth of our grief at the death of a loved-one.

My promise to those who read this book is that it is all my truth and I believe it will assist all who read it. Even if you do not agree with every word of the book, I hope exploring your own views and beliefs with an open mind will be a further inspiration to you.

In questioning our current beliefs I do not suggest they are wrong. All faith that promotes brotherhood, love, peace, charity and harmony has my full support. I encourage everyone to keep with their own faith, if it works for them, whilst remaining curious and respectful of others' beliefs.

To promote clear communication, I have prepared a Glossary, located conveniently at the very back of the book for easy reference. Definitions vary slightly, so it may be helpful to refer to the glossary so you interpret the words as they are written.

How to read this book: Read it slowly and make a commitment to read it all. I have tackled a huge subject, the picture of the world we pass into when we die gradually builds through the book, it is therefore important to read it all, in the sequence that it is presented. Reading the end first is not advised as the end only makes sense after consideration is given to the beginning and the middle - like most things in life.

As you read try to picture, in your mind's eye, the situation of the ghost from his point of view, feel how they must experience their world. Most of all, be aware of their reasoning and sense how poorly prepared they were for the change of dimension when they died and wonder if we can become better ready to die and be *"Dead Happy"*.

Also, attempt to suspend your judgment, put your critical mind to one side, as you read. Pretend it's all true and assess everything at the end, once you've allowed yourself to really see and hold this point of view. At the end I'll summarise the viewpoints and discuss typical questions to make your assessment easier when you finish the book.

Please enjoy sharing these views, after you finish the book, you'll be better equipped for death and for life. Even if you don't agree with the views, you'll be able to debate some of these topical subjects: the existence and nature of ghosts, hell, heaven, spirits and poltergeists.

Two

MOST GHOSTS DON'T KNOW THAT THEY'RE DEAD

One of the funniest, yet most tragic, things I've learnt about ghosts is that they don't believe they are ghosts. So in an ironic sense, they don't believe in ghosts either.

How can that be? How can someone be a ghost and not know that they are dead?

Sounds ridiculous, but it's true. Many books support this theory and the ghosts I've chatted with bear out this truth too.

So how could we die and not know about it? When we fall asleep nothing actually happens that we are aware of. We're tired, relaxed, then the next thing we know, we've been to sleep and are now awake. Even if you keep dozing off on those rare occasions when you have a lie-in, you are only aware of having woken up. How often have you said, or heard it said, "I must have dropped off"? Or even when people think that they have not been to sleep at all, "I was just resting my eyes" yet everyone in the room heard the snoring!

Why should the deeper sleep of death be any different? If you talk to people about relatives dying they often say he seemed so peaceful and he went so quietly. Yes people do also just nod off to death. This is quite reasonable really, if you think about it.

A book that I shall refer to is called 'The Return of Arthur Conan Doyle' and includes some of the teaching passed on by the late Arthur Conan Doyle through a medium during a two year period. In this book he says "Everyone does not at once realise that he has passed out of his physical body." He expands on that and later says "Not that there will be anything novel about our astral environment, since we go there every night when we fall asleep. Sleep being a little death, we are well practiced in dying, and in this fashion die three hundred and sixty-five times yearly. With each day we awake. With the same certainty we shall presently awake after our death, since both sleeping and dying are natural functions of our being."

Sudden death is a more shocking concept to take in I agree, you may wonder how we could miss the experience of dying in an accident. But consider a case where after an accident where the victim loses consciousness and wakes up in hospital saying "Where am I? What happened?". Death could also happen during the same state of unconsciousness and you can see how we could be unaware of it.

Think about it though and keep an open mind while I share an example from a book by Carl Wickland, a psychiatrist. He wrote about his mental patients, and his wife's experiences as a medium, over a thirty year period. There will be more about his book 'Thirty Years Amongst The Dead' later.

There was the ghost of a Blacksmith chatting through the medium, Mrs Wickland, back in the 1920's who seemed surprised to hear that he was dead. He went on to remark that "I was just shoeing this horse and got a bump on my head, it must've been harder than I thought".

How often have you hurt yourself so severely that you've gone into a state of shock and become almost oblivious to your surroundings and even unaware of the pain you felt? If you consider that the state of shock is completely available after death due to sudden accident then it's easier to imagine how people die and simply miss the experience. Next thing they know they're up and about, rubbing their sore head but apart from that they're ok except that their body is still in the morgue, the ambulance or the hospital bed.

So, please accept for a moment that this is all possible, however incredible or far fetched it may seem. We'll be looking at evidence later but for now just accept it as possible and we can follow the idea further to give you even better value from your book.

I am not saying that this is true of all death, please appreciate that I am talking about what may happen and often has happened to someone who becomes a ghost. Most people do not become ghosts, as far as I know.

To help us consider what it is like for these dead people who think they are still alive, let's look at the example of a man who got run down by a car when he was crossing the road.

Suddenly hit by a car and killed instantly the man gets up (and out of his body) rubs his head and thinks "that was close, gosh my head hurts".

Off he goes walking along as he was, on his way home. When he gets in, his family seem a bit strange. They are all upset and crying. His meal isn't even ready and what's more, none of them talk to him. He wonders what he's done wrong and eventually when he can think of nothing to deserve this, he asks his wife.

"What have I done wrong?"

She ignores him. He wishes she'd stop crying and tell him what's going on. Instead she prepares dinner but cooks him nothing, doesn't even set a place at the table for him, no coffee, nothing.

So our friend is pretty upset himself, he loves his family and hates to see them so miserable, destitute even. He goes to bed and sleeps with his wife who sobs most of the night and refuses to talk.

In the morning he awakes with renewed optimism, "maybe they'll have got over it" he thinks. No such luck, he comes down for breakfast and the same story. Loads of sad red eyes and still even his kids won't speak to him.

"Stuff you" he says "I'm going to work".

At work, they know he's dead too and when he gets there he is horrified to find someone else in his office using his desk and doing his job.

"What's going on? This is my office" but no answer. More people ignore him. He goes to his boss who ignores him, even though they were good friends, which adds to the anger and confusion. But of course the boss cannot see or hear the ghost of his employee. Now he's going demented with worry and confusion, his whole world is shattered. His family, his colleagues, even his friends don't acknowledge him.

The confusion grows and he becomes more worried with every incident. The harder this man looks for the answer the further from it he gets. He only looks amongst the material world he knew. So he's a ghost: A spirit attached to the dimension of being in a material form.

What now? What can this ghost do? He wants to be acknowledged, we all do. We all want friends and communication, love, respect, all those things this ghost wants too. He feels entitled to all those enjoyable feelings he had before. He thinks he's alive but is beginning to think he must have done something awful to be treated like this.

He starts to wander around the place, trying to speak to anyone who'll listen, but no one does. If he learns to, maybe he'll smash things to attract attention and still be ignored. This is one unhappy state to experience.

There is even a recorded example of a ghost describing how he "got on the bus and this fat lady sat on top of me. I bashed and bashed her, shouted at her but she wouldn't get off me. The bus came to my stop and still she sat there ignoring me. I passed my stop. Eventually she got up and got off the bus."

The ghost still thinks that he has a body and experiences a feeling of being pinned down when sat on. He does not realise that he could simply move away by thinking he's somewhere else. he thinks that he still has a body and can only get up when the large weight is removed.

Ghosts that open doors, in a haunted house for example, are exhibiting the same phenomena, they think they have a body and can therefore only enter a room by opening the door or by waiting for someone else (mortal) to open it.

One ghost, Frank, who spoke through the medium, Mrs Wickland, said "I don't know what is the matter with me anyhow. I have asked everybody I saw, but everybody passed by; they were so stuck up they wouldn't talk to a fellow any more".

Frank's comment shows the way in which a confused ghost will blame other people for his condition of being ignored. He'll hardly find the solution by blaming us, living mortals, for ignoring him will he? He's the one who has no body, how can it be our fault? He spends his time thinking we are ignoring him, if only he could realise that we cannot see him.

The state of confusion is vast. It's greater than anything I can think of in our lives and impossible to understand should you get like Frank. Frank had been so confused that he had been influencing a mental patient, Mrs Burton and his exorcism from her, along with other spirits, was part of the cure of her mental difficulty.

Eventually, after what can be hundreds of years or just months, something seems to happen to awaken these lost souls. Some wander around and find a receptive person and take over their body, yes possess them, it's more common than you may think and not as extreme as in films like 'The Exorcist'. We will look at possession in a later section. For now let's look at other options.

Maybe the ghost will accept that his only way to communicate is to smash vases around people's homes. He forgets the joy of having a family and he accepts his tragic situation as the only reality he is now entitled to.

To attract people's attention he makes a noise or moves things. This is called a 'poltergeist' or noisy ghost. Unfortunately this merely proves that he exists and that we do seem to ignore him unless he is a nuisance. It could make things worse for the poltergeist, as now he believes even more firmly that he's alive and therefore is less able to realise that he's died.

So he becomes a Poltergeist. He smashes things for attention. All he really wants is to be acknowledged and loved, just like you and me. We don't like being ignored or excluded, especially by those we love. Why should a ghost need anything different?

I've heard many theories about poltergeists, one of which is that they are common in the homes of adolescent girls. Some therefore suggest that this must be a phenomena generated by the adolescent girls. I propose that the upset and ignored ghost can find empathy with the rebellious nature of some adolescents and enjoys being around them. You would surely want to change the world yourself if you were a ghost, ignored and unloved for some years.

You can see, if you are willing to experiment by accepting this philosophy as true, that it is pretty hard to imagine the dead person ever getting out of his confused state on his own.

So, what can be done to solve his problem? What I call a rescue, to rescue him from his tragic reality and expand him to a more enjoyable and appropriate reality.

Through mediums, I have spoken to ghosts like the example and sensed both their state of sadness and then their elation at finding a new life with joy, love and communication with their family, albeit with those family members who are already dead. The witnessing of the transformation of a ghost, believing he's alive, to the discovery of his immortality and of the presence of the spirit world, is so moving that I am determined to help prevent us mortals entering that state of confusion and often loneliness.

To conclude this part, most ghosts are people who don't think that they're dead and as they often don't believe in ghosts they would not consider their death as a possible explanation for their peculiar state of existence. They just think like the example Frank, from Wickland's book, that people are "too stuck up to talk to a fellow any more" or that they must be being punished for something they've done.

The answer to their problem becomes harder for them to find as each moment goes by. Just as we tend to rationalise our experience so that we see ourselves as mostly in the right, so a ghost will rationalise his own experience and blame us all for ignoring him, rather than seeking an explanation beyond his existing beliefs.

We'll look at the solution to their ghost state in a later section on rescue work, a rescue being a term for the way ghosts are enlightened as to their state or rescued from their confusion.

Three

SPIRITS SHOW THEMSELVES FOR SOME GOOD REASON

So we accept that a ghost is a dead person, who doesn't know it yet, as he thinks he is still alive with a mortal body

Let's look at Spirits, who are (in my view) non-mortal entities (people) who know their state as not having a body. As such they have an extra awareness that we are denied or deny ourselves by having our material form. So the spirit knows that he's a spirit and a ghost thinks he's alive (with a body).

Even if you don't agree with my distinction between Spirits and Ghosts please follow this definition, as it will help me express myself and give you value for money from your book.

While we are considering definitions, it is widely believed that some spirits have the job of watching over us and helping us with our mortal lives. I call these spirits 'spirit guides' although some of you may feel that these are your 'guardian angels'.

Earlier I said that most ghosts think they're not dead. Well, now I want to consider Spirits that some people see and why they show themselves to us. If you got the idea about Ghosts being unaware of being dead and feeling ignored then it's easy to imagine how a ghost would want to be seen and to communicate with his family, friends or his boss. What of these Spirits, what are they after when we see them?

Well, it would be a staggering claim to make that I could understand what Spirits do or why. I recognise a certain distinction between our experience of ghosts with those of Spirits and would not be so impertinent to you or the Spirits to claim a full knowledge.

I have come to a certain sense of knowing, however humble, and wish to share that with you as it will serve a purpose later.

My theory is that when we see a ghost, either it's a ghost (as previously defined) or it's a Spirit. If it's a spirit then it's performing some helpful function as these Spirits do not seem to want to do evil or mischief. They do not feel lost or confused and are not compelled through loneliness to seek our attention.

What functions are performed by Spirits? Who knows? Again I cannot know the full range of 'Their' expertise and do not presume to. However their role and influence over our lives will unfold a little as this book progresses. For now though, let's take one step at a time.

One function of Spirits showing themselves is to help us by drawing attention to things in our lives so we may have or avoid an experience.

Another function is to help the poor ghosts. In an example coming later a ghost is rescued from his state of confusion (as a ghost) as a direct result of someone seeing not the ghost but a Spirit who showed herself to draw attention to the haunting of the house. The home-owner assumed that the lady they saw was the ghost but it was one of their Spirit Guides. If the Spirit hadn't been seen there would have been no rescue attempt made for the ghost. Hence the reason for the original vision having occurred.

So if you see a ghost it's either a ghost in the sense of someone who doesn't know that he's dead, or it's a Spirit showing itself consciously for some good purpose.

What are dead people like?

Now from our earlier look at the idea of a ghost, you can imagine that some are pretty sad. They are lonely and confused, can be really missing communication and often feel ignored and mistreated by their friends and family. Remember they are being ignored? So some are very sad and lonely.

Some are a bit like people with bodies, confused but blissfully ignorant of their confusion. These ones can be happy or sad and often they are quite bored, as they have been doing the same things for a long time and things happen to them that seem beyond their control, for they have not learnt to control their environment. How could they influence a material world, if they think they've got a body and haven't? They often just drift around the place.

Ghosts can also retain a strong element of their previous characteristics, so they are very much as they were in their bodies. If they were happy and mischievous pranksters, so they may remain when spoken with.

There will be examples of some different types of ghost later in the book.

Spirits, on the other hand, knowing they are dead, have an understanding of the world and they seem to want to help the universe. They are kind, benevolent and full of love and a will to help.

They have their own personalities and idiosyncrasies, as you will see, and in many cases that may include a sense of humour and enjoyment. There have been very few spirits in my experience who are solemn, most seem cheerful and sympathetic to the problems of ghosts and those suffering in their mortal lives.

How can you tell if you drop off to death?

So now we have established the theory that we can just nod off to death and not notice, let's assume that is the case and move on. If we can die without our knowing, it's very important to devise a method that proves we are alive, or a way to tell when we are dead.

We are often taught many things that we should expect to see when we die, from St Peter's pearly gates to winged angels. I have it on good authority, from a spirit with a great sense of humour, that the pearly gates were taken down centuries ago, because St. Peter got so bored hanging around waiting for people to die!

For many people, after they die, if they do not see what they expect then they must still be alive. Until they hear the trumpets of angels they must still have a body. I will build on this idea as you read on.

From what you have already read, you will be able to realise that you are dead if your family and friends all ignore you. If everyone seems to be unaware of your existence, you will be prompted to wonder if you've died. You may recognise that the people you cared about most are grieving, it could be your death that makes them so sad.

What should you expect when you die?

From the reading that I've done into the experience of dying, it sounds just like waking up in friendly surroundings, amidst old friends. The descriptions given by people who have been classified dead, perhaps when their heart stopped, and recovered have given charming pictures of a friendly white light and of feeling full of love and comfort.

Some say they saw their old friends and family around their bedside, waiting to greet them and take them into the next world. Others say they heard a voice telling them it wasn't time for them to die and that they should go back.

If you want my suggestion, keep an open mind and do not expect any particular thing to happen, otherwise you could fall into the same situation of believing that you are alive, with a body, because you haven't seen a bright white light and you could become a confused ghost.

It is interesting reading the various tales from people who have almost died, some titles are included in the book-list at the back of this book. This is looked at in further detail in the section titled 'The Pearly Gates'.

Four

HOW TO DEAL WITH GHOSTS

This section deals with the art of explaining to a ghost that he has died in such a way that he will accept his new situation and open his mind to a new reality or world. This is a sort of 'ghost therapy' and great consideration and compassion has to be employed to win the confidence of the ghost and establish a credible rapport with him.

Whilst I shall explain the technique, I must advise great caution in embarking too readily to seek out opportunities to practice ghost therapy at hauntings. I find this all very simple, almost automatic, having done this sort of ghost therapy for years. Even so, every now and then I am reminded that some ghosts can be quite tricky and "naughty" (as you'll read later in this book), testing my intuition and experience. So be very careful, some ghosts will pretend that they are whoever you are seeking, just for the pleasure of being able to talk to someone. Other ghosts will give startling predictions to please an audience and hold their attention, just as a naughty ghost said I had six months to live over twenty years ago.

You can perhaps imagine the shock of being told that you are dead. Often a ghost will argue, because he feels as alive as ever, sometimes more so and he may really believe he has a body.

The process is referred to here and by many as 'rescuing' the ghost, presumably the term has evolved as the ghost is rescued from a state of confusion or from being tied to the earth world.

I call it an art, because there is much skill in understanding the condition of someone you cannot necessarily see or hear. Great perception and intuition are required, in addition to other skills and techniques which can be learnt.

Some of these techniques are shown in later examples, but be aware that there is more to it than this book will cover. This book is not intended as a manual for the dabbler, so it will not attempt to teach all the skills required to do rescue work but it will show how to resolve hauntings.

Rescue: what is a rescue?

If you've read the earlier part of the book then you're ready for this chapter, if you haven't then I suggest you go back and read it. If you don't agree with the first part of the book, then I suggest that you read this chapter as though you do accept that it's another possibility and decide what you want to believe for yourself later, once you've finished the whole book. If you read like this, with an open mind, then you'll probably enjoy yourself more and get better value from your book.

Rescue is simply an expression for the process of helping a ghost to understand what his experience is and helping him to understand that he has died and is now a Spirit. An important part of this rescue process is to do this safely by helping this new Spirit find his way into the dimension to which he can go.

It's not good enough in my experience just to shove someone away saying "You're dead now buzz off". To me this is not a rescue as the ghost may not have got the message and may simply regard you as crackers and go off and play somewhere else.

A rescue can take many forms and we will explore some of those as we progress through the subject. Initially I will give an example of a common format and one that took place at a seance I attended some years ago but relates to all of the ones I've experienced.

Basically a ghost is at the seance, often communicating through a medium but unaware that he is using another's body. Often the ghost is really pleased to be speaking to people sometimes for the first time in ages. Some are quite cross that they are at a seance as their previous religious upbringing and belief frowned on such things.

Here goes:

Rescue example.

This is a record of a seance that took place in the 1980's and there was a medium and in addition the group used a table to aid communication. With their hands placed lightly on the table, it would move according to the message of the spirit. The table would tilt and knock back onto all of its legs, three times for yes, two for no and could run through the alphabet using, for example, six knocks for F, seven for G.

The table is a valuable aid to a medium who may be unsure of the message. A medium can be male or female, I've met both and for the sake of brevity the male gender is used here to accommodate both. If the message doesn't make sense to the medium, he can always check that he's got it right, through the use of the table.

The energy in the room changed as the medium sensed the ghost and said,

"God bless you friend"

The table was still, but so still, it was rigid as if fixed to the floor.

"Can we know you?"

"No." Two knocks of the table for No, it would be three for Yes. It often amused us when we asked if there was someone else who wanted to communicate with us after a guide had gone, and the table moved to say NO, there was no one there!

"God bless you friend, how are things with you, do you wish to say something?" we asked.

"No"

"Well we care about you friend, are things a bit odd?" We asked this as we had come to know how confused some people became when they were speaking to a group of people at a seance, often something they had disapproved of in their material lives.

"Yes"

"Have people been ignoring you?"

"Yes".

"Are you looking for someone?"

"Yes" again the table knocked very positively three times for yes.

"Do you know you have passed over?"

This may seem a strange question to you. How could anyone not know they're dead? Easy, believe me, it is amazing how many people come through at a seance thinking they have just had a bump on the head or have just woken up in the wrong place after a deep sleep.

"No"

"Well, God bless you friend. You have passed over, that's why things seem, different. Have you been trying to speak to relatives who don't seem to hear you? Do they all seem very sad?"

"Yes, yes!"

"Well friend, you've stepped out of your body and are on the other side. Didn't you think it was odd the way you were talking to us?"

"Yes"

"If you want to be helped to adjust to the world you're now in, it's easy; just think of a friend or relative who has already passed over, a grandparent or anyone like that. Are you willing to give it a try, what have you got to lose?"

"Yes, I'll try anything"

"Then open your mind, look around you and think of your loved ones.... Do you see them?"

Even as we asked the question we could sense a loosening of the vibration in the table, a lightening of the atmosphere. The table didn't move.

Then suddenly, "Yes, I see them".

"Is it someone you knew, someone you trust?" we asked.

"Yes, it's my mother, she died when I was born."

"God bless you friend" with tears of joy in our eyes "go with her and good luck."

"Thank you" the ghost said as it left.

What is going on at a rescue?

In a Rescue all that is happening is the opening of the mind or eyes of a ghost to a dimension that is available to him, which he has not looked at before. A ghost is so locked into the material world that he does not even look around him. It's like not being able to see the wood for the trees but only with more serious and frustrating consequences.

It has been suggested through mediums, that once dead we are approached by dead friends and relatives who come to our side to 'help us over'. In near death experiences written about in such books as 'Life After Life' (by Raymond A Moody Jr MD) this is described as friends and family waiting and most who have spoken of their experience talk of a sort of a bright white light. Read these books for yourself though, and form your own opinion, there are several available listed at the end of this book.

Well these dead friends and relatives are pretty frustrated when they are trying to attract the attention of their friend, who has just died, who denies his death to such an extent that he does not see them. If he's been a bad person he may even try not to see them as he may expect to go to Hell and eternal damnation, so he may avoid that at all cost.

So the basic ingredient of a good rescue is to convince the ghost he's dead and ask him to look around for friends and relatives who have already died. Once the ghost sees his relatives he'll also hear them and be in conversation about going with them so the mortal rescuer's job is done.

Because I am not Clairvoyant or Clairaudient and therefore cannot see or hear a ghost directly, I find an effective Rescue practice is to make it clear to the ghost that I cannot see him or hear him and use this to emphasise my belief that he has died and must be a ghost. I also ask if things have been a bit confusing, as I know that most ghosts are very confused. I ask if he has been ignored a great deal, possibly by people he loved. Very few ghosts disagree with these ideas, they believe that I must know what I'm talking about because it's often the first thing they've heard that makes any sense of their present condition.

Also I often ask them to think of an accident or illness, could they have died? With a bit of thought, now that they are open minded and less fearful they can often remember that they were ill, had been run over or kicked by a horse for example.

Once they reach this stage of understanding then I consider that they are ready to open their spiritual eyes to their new reality and I ask them to think of their loved ones who have died before them. Often I suggest thinking of a Grandmother, a Grandfather or even a Great Grandparent, because I want the ghost to turn their attention to a deceased relative – not someone still alive.

Once our ghost agrees to think of such a dead friend or relative, almost instantly they see them and the room is filled with joyful psychic energy.

In all the rescues I've attended and participated in, I have never known this method to fail: once they're willing to 'go over', each ghost has been greeted by someone they know or someone friendly who takes them into the other dimension. Some cases, however, are quite tricky and can test the skill of the rescuer. The only difficulty, at the time of writing, has been with Patrick, whose situation is dealt with later in the book.

Sometimes the spirit who leads the ghost to the 'other side' is someone who had been wronged by the ghost in their mortal lives and the ghost is initially afraid when he sees that person. Once the two can see each other however, it seems that the ghost can also hear the assurance of the spirit and quickly loses fear, knowing that the spirit wants to lead him from confusion to safety.

Rescue then, in a Spiritual sense, is when a ghost is rescued from his confused state and brought to one of enlightenment, where he is able to focus attention on the 'spiritual dimension' rather than being stuck in our material world.

I used to attend my regular weekly seance and we performed Rescues almost every week. Ghosts would be brought into the seance or circle by our spirit guides, or the ghosts own guides, and would speak through the Medium. We would explain their situation, just as I have described. The same method has been used for many years and is clearly documented by Wickland in 1926.

What amazes me, is that Wickland was doing this way back in 1908 for thirty years and still we are, as a society, completely ignorant about the subject of ghosts, exorcism and possession. I hope this book helps to shake all that fear and prejudice off the subject so we can get on and treat it properly.

So what's going on? That's what I used to ask. How come all these lost, dead people come through our humble circle totally confused, often after being dead for years? They sometimes describe how they hung around their wife, long after she was a widow, not knowing they were dead and wondering why she wouldn't listen.

Incredible, but true!

Even in a traumatic accident, people have got up, brushed themselves down and walked away, leaving their body behind. They don't even know they died! If you've seen the film 'Ghost' with Patrick Swazye and Demi Moore, you may recall the part where 'Sam Wheat' gets killed by the mugger and doesn't notice. He runs after his own killer with such determination that he didn't notice his own death. It is only when he sees 'Molly' crying over his own dead body, that he realises he had been killed by the mugger. 'Ghost' is a great film which shows such a valid picture of one death experience, so close to the truth I've come to accept.

So when we help someone find their way we call it a Rescue and there are many of these 'Rescue Circles' going on all over the world. We help the ghost notice the absence of his body and get him to accept his death and discover the new dimension that he can go to.

It's great to help, but it upsets me that it's necessary to help these people. The situation should not be possible where we can die and not understand what's going on. By now, in the 20th century, we should know better. We should be better educated or at least, better informed.

So, that's the idea of this book. Even if you don't agree with any of this, if you read it now as though you believe it, you will be able to call on the method and try it if your world seems funny. You'll be able to consider that maybe you've died.

After a bump on the head or a long sleep and the whole world seems peculiar where everyone ignores you, consider whether they see you or not.

You may have had a harder bump than you know.

Five

MY FIRST HAUNTING

Sitting and Rescue work: my first time.

So how did this all come my way? Well read on and I'll tell you, it was a real surprise to me.

Heather, the office secretary one day just came right out with it.

"Lance, you know a few people, do you know anyone who could help some friends of mine? They've got a ghost."

You can imagine my surprise, but also my curiosity and I was interested. Four years earlier I had met a married couple, Tony and Patricia who were Spiritualists and I had investigated their beliefs and these people had become good friends. I had eventually accepted that the Spiritualists seemed to have some valid answers to many of life's mysteries and seemed to know the way life really is. I read messages from wise Red Indians transcribed at seances and saw how they never contradicted any part of the Bible or another religion I knew of.

To me it seemed just like an update of ancient philosophies and teaching. This was a way in which we could chat to wise old Spirits and get a philosophy for life in modern language. It seemed more logical to me than some things I'd been told in Religious Instruction at school I can tell you. Also why depend on such old and often translated material, when it seemed possible to get an update from the same source?

Having accepted that this was the way, I really knew that one day I'd 'get into this'. I sort of felt it in my bones and knew I had to wait until the time was right.

So, was this a sign? This story from Heather, was it put in my way to be a catalyst for my future involvement in helping others through Spiritualism? I don't know, but this is what happened.

Heather described the trouble the family were having. The details of the haunting included the owner seeing a female ghost, who was tall and serene in a long flowing robe. The family's two children, sensing a presence on the landing, refused to leave their bedroom at night which had resulted in bed-wetting, a habit which they'd previously outgrown.

I went to visit my Spiritualist friends and described all Heather had told me and asked what they thought.

"We're sitting tonight, why don't you join us and we'll ask what to do. Come round at seven o'clock, don't drink any alcohol before you come round."

Even though I wasn't sure what sitting actually involved, wild horses couldn't have held me back! I knew it was some sort of a seance. I had an image of a dark room with flickering candle flames, but I wanted to go all the same.

We sat round the little table, lights on, no candlelight, no whispering and just chatted. Tony explained what would happen, that following some opening prayers we would each place our hands on the table and that it would tilt and then rock back into a normal position to tap on the ground. These taps or knocks on the floor would be taken to mean something. He explained "three taps for yes, two for no and the letters of the alphabet can be tapped out, ie one for A, two for B". Tony explained that this adds to our own clairvoyance so that if we think we have the message in our heads, the tapping of the table can serve to confirm our impression or put us right if we are incorrect.

Tony also explained that sometimes one of the people sitting round the table, one of us, may get an idea come into their head of what the message may be. The table will then tilt towards that person to encourage them to share their thoughts, so the message can be confirmed by a simple "yes" through three taps of the table. This can speed up communication and encourage a person to share an idea, however ridiculous it may seem, a sort of psychic prompt.

Then once the instructions were over, we said the Lord's Prayer and Tony said a prayer for guidance and protection and asked the Spirit Guides to help those troubled and to see if we could help those friends of Heather's. (Some people have asked me about the reason for prayer at these meetings and this will be discussed later in this book).

The table tilted, two of its legs lifted slowly and tapped back down to the floor. This seemed to be taken as a signal that a spirit had arrived. It certainly amazed me, my hands were on the table and it felt as though it was indeed being moved by someone other than the three of us sitting round it.

"God bless you." Tony smiled as he spoke, apparently pleased to feel the presence of a friend. He seemed to recognise the way the table moved. It is strange but no two spirits move the table the with the same vigour or pace, some even tilt it in different directions. Each individual is consistent yet they can still express hesitation and firmness.

For example when they've made a statement through the table we might innocently say "Are you sure?". The table will bash three times to say YES very definitely. I suppose it's a bit insolent of us to question those spirits who can see how things are a lot better than us!

"God bless you" came the answer.

"Is that the Senator?" A regular at their circle, The Senator was their door keeper and often controlled the circle, guarding against mischievous spirits and making sure each spirit waited his turn to 'speak'.

"Yes".

So it went on, messages from loved ones, practical advice for the children. A warm welcome was offered to me, for which I gave my thanks. I was pretty amazed by this time. The way the table was moving was really uncanny.

"Can you help the friends in distress?" Tony asked, once the formalities were over.

"Yes" was the Spirit Guide's answer.

We were advised to go to the house and hold next week's circle there. "Take some freesias with you, they'll help you".

It sounded heavy to me, going round to see a ghost with a bunch of flowers. Crazy as it was, I decided to go. The others seemed so confident, no sign of fear.

To close the circle we prayed again closing with a verse that Tony and Patricia always said after removing their hands from the table.

"Dear friends,

Keep us safe this night

Secure from all our fears,

May angels guide us while we sleep

'Till morning light appears."

After the close of the seance, or sitting, we sat and chatted together. I was asking the questions, trying to understand more of the experience I'd just had and asking for more information about Tony and Patricia's work with the Spirits.

I was excited to hear more of the practical side of a belief that I had accepted so many years before and especially to discover the value of rescue work.

Tony and Patricia told me that six months before, they had been told by their Spirit Guides that someone else would be joining their circle. The only clue they were given regarding the newcomer's name was the letter 'L'.

It had been so long since I'd seen them, that they had forgotten my interest in Spiritualism and they hadn't been able to think of anyone called 'L', who may join them. They told me that they had been very amused when I had telephoned and told them Teresa's story. So here was Lance, joining their group.

Next week, off we went to visit the haunted house taking a small bunch of freesias with us. I drove, I was a bit apprehensive but of course tried not to show it.

The Haunting

The three of us arrived at the so called 'haunted house' and I introduced everyone and we found a vase for the freesias.

Tony set up the small table and after arranging the chairs around it, we sat down.

Tony chatted briefly to explain that we would first say the Lord's Prayer together then he would say a brief prayer asking for protection of our small group. Tony also explained about the use of the table to tap out messages when our clairvoyance was unclear or we needed confirmation of some detail. There were no questions and whilst still apprehensive we all seemed as relaxed as we could be.

The prayers said, we all sat with hands on the table to concentrate our minds.

Almost immediately the table moved, almost a bow, just one slow movement lifting two legs as it tilted towards Patricia, and then back onto the floor.

Remarkable though this may seem, it was possible to recognise from that one movement of the table that The Senator, the usual table guide of the circle, was communicating with us.

"God bless you, is that The Senator?" Tony asked, seeking confirmation of what he already sensed.

"Yes" The table knocked three times in his inimitable way.

"Is everything in order for us to continue?" Tony keen to check our state of readiness and probably to raise the confidence of the home owners who had wanted to get our help.

All was well so we thanked The Senator who went quiet to give space for the session to begin.

Without a delay Patricia began to adopt a hunched, almost frightened posture, her whole body curled up over the table. She began to sniff, almost sobbing. I was a little concerned and glanced at Tony, who was calm and seemed really confident not at all bothered that his wife was becoming so distressed. He inspired such confidence that I was able to remain relaxed.

"God bless you friend" said Tony in the direction of his wife.

"I didn't do it" came a sad, quiet, frightened and pathetic voice from Patricia.

"I didn't do it" she said repeatedly, the voice pleaded to be believed.

We assured the ghost communicating through Patricia, the medium, that we were friends and that he was safe.

After a while of comforting and reassuring the ghost, his story became clear. This was a tragic case.

The person we spoke with had been a Village Idiot perhaps a hundred years before, the subject of local mockery, a sort of outcast but fed almost for the entertainment of the villagers.

His only playmate had been a girl of around three years old, probably a similar mental age and without adult prejudices against the retarded man.

One day the girl was tragically found dead in a field and the villagers assumed that the village idiot had killed her.

Stoning the man to death in a dark woodshed had been the villagers' instant justice and they were unable to hear or believe the gentle, frightened voice of the man saying "I didn't do it".

So for perhaps a hundred years this sad figure, who was misunderstood throughout his life, had been drifting around since his death. He was still hunched up, in the defensive position, to protect himself from the stoning he remembered, still sobbing the feeble message "I didn't do it". I didn't do it."

For why would he kill the only friend he'd ever had? It must have seemed so strange to his simple mind, all so confusing.

We spoke with "the idiot" and told him he was safe, we believed him and if he looked up and around him, he'd see that things were different and that he was safe.

After a while as we held his hands (the medium's) the sad figure uncurled his cowering body and began to look up.

Tears fell from that sad face and then smiled as the village idiot saw his old playmate, the three year old skipping round the room.

"Do you see someone you know?" Tony asked sensing the joy in our friend.

"Yes"

"Is it your old playmate?" Tony asked correctly guessing the identity of the Spiritual visitor.

"Go with her, she'll help you understand and show you where to go" Tony urged.

The idiot and his playmate left and all was quiet for a few moments, Patricia returned from her trance and with a tissue restored her face.

The Senator came through and made comments on what had occurred for the owners of the so called haunted house.

The family living in the haunted house had been disturbed by the presence of the Village Idiot. The children had sensed his presence and were concerned by the sadness and would not wish to go onto the landing. The children's mother, hadn't seen a ghost but had in fact seen one of her Spirit Guides who was coming close to the family to protect them and by showing herself she motivated the family to get help.

The Senator said the flowers had been for the Village Idiot, a comforting smell of the outdoors, which would reassure him. The Senator also explained, as he did often, that in such a Spiritual Rescue not only is the one with whom we communicate helped but also there are many watching. He described it as if we were in Wembley Stadium, "It may seem like a lounge to you but it's as if you are in the middle of a football stadium with thousands of Spirits all crowded round to see what's going on". He explained that when we get the message through to the one ghost, the thousands watching also get the idea and also move on to the Spirit World.

So, our work done we thanked the Spirit people for their guidance and with our usual prayer closed the circle. We then had coffee a chat and left, without the flowers. Incidentally, Patricia knew nothing of what had happened whilst she had been in a clairvoyant trance. All she was aware of through all this was an overwhelming fragrance of the freesias and can still remember nothing else. We told her what had happened and she was delighted to have been of use.

Following this experience I did join their circle as predicted six months earlier. We met every week and performed many rescues, helping ghost after ghost to find the way to the Spirit World. We always opened with the Lord's Prayer and the Protection Prayer. Time was also given for meditation to assist each of us in the work of developing our psychic skills or Spiritual gifts, as many people call them.

It was during this period when I was attending the weekly sittings, that I discovered that ghosts will sometimes follow me around, if they think I'll be able to help them. The following story is just one example of how this can happen.

Six

GHOSTS CAN EAVESDROP

Back in April 1980 I was at a loose end one Sunday and went to spend the day with a friend who lived round the corner. We decided to leave our Hertfordshire home for the day and jumped aboard my friend's old banger and drove up to London to visit his sister and future brother-in-law. A warm welcome awaited us at the door of their London apartment. It was one of those large two storey flats in a vast four or five floor building; originally a large house, Alice and Paul occupied the ground and first floors.

After making a fuss of their 'thousand and one' Dalmatian puppies, we were invited to the sumptuous upstairs lounge for coffee.

Pleasant conversation relaxed us as we sank deep into the chairs.

"By the way, we've got a ghost." Said Alice.

"Really? Tell us about it" I replied, sitting forward in my chair. Not frightened, but fascinated, interested to know why Alice seemed so relaxed and proud of the revelation.

Alice explained that every so often, she thought about once a month, the door of the very room we occupied would open mysteriously, on its own. Then she described how another door would open and close on the other side of the room as though someone had walked through the room and out again.

They never saw anyone, just the opening and closing of doors. You may know the really solid wooden doors of these Edwardian high ceiling homes, they don't open on their own. Alice added that sometimes papers would be brushed aside on the table as though someone had walked passed.

"We don't mind having a ghost," said Alice, "in fact we quite like it".

"What a waste of time. You'd think whoever it is would have better things to do with himself, rather than wandering in and out of here!" I expressed myself sincerely, sharing my belief that ghosts are lost spirits who would be better off living new lives, not hanging around with us!

After much chat and more coffee, we returned home to Hertfordshire and back to our routines.

On Monday at the usual meeting with my friends, we enjoyed friendly conversation, jokes and good humour as we prepared for the circle, arranging the chairs and the table. We said the Lord's Prayer, then a prayer for protection and on with the circle. After a greeting from the Spirit Guides, including the Senator, who came as usual to oversee our humble circle, another spirit was introduced.

"God bless you" we welcomed the stranger.

"God bless you"

"Do we know you?" we asked.

The table moved, by tilting towards me.

"Hello, how do I know you?" I asked.

The table moved through the alphabet, you know, one knock for A, twice for B and our clairvoyant member Patricia completing the message. She likes her inspiration to be confirmed in this way. After a little while the story unfolded. Our spirit friend knew me, having listened to what I said about him the previous day at Alice and Paul's apartment.

Yes, he was the Ghost. He agreed that visiting the London apartment did seem a waste of time but he'd been there once a month since the end of the second world war.

Apparently he and his brother had been called to arms and had been at the house in London, just before going to war. On parting, their final words to each other "see you here after the war", were never forgotten by our visitor. He'd simply been looking for his brother ever since.

He had followed me to the circle as it was the first time anyone had said anything that sounded hopeful to him, likely to help his search. He agreed that hanging around the apartment once a month had been fruitless and a waste of time.

Our regular Guide, The Senator, located the lost brother. Would you believe he was still on the battle field, still fighting the war long after he had been shot dead? He had died and not noticed, so he carried on fighting the hundreds of other soldiers who had died and not realised it.

With the advice of our guide we all prayed, trying to reunite the long lost brothers. How sad I felt, so depressed at the thought that even after giving his life for freedom and his country the poor man could be suffering a battle, the fear and confusion for another forty odd years.

We sat quietly and thought of the brother still at war.

Elation! The whole room seemed alive with joy and celebration. They had found each other and you could sense the relief, the atmosphere was electric.

Thank you, the brothers said, but we'd really enjoyed helping them and felt privileged that they'd shared their experience with us. We should have thanked them for the joy of their love, which we had all sensed.

Seven

GHOSTBUSTING – RESCUE WORK

The Priest Rescue

At a rescue circle, after several successful rescues and communications with guiding spirits, another ghost, lost soul or confused spirit 'came through' to communicate.

"God bless you, friend" we greeted our new guest.

"God Bless You" came the almost stern reply.

"Do we know you friend?" we asked, a quick way to assess the state of any new visitor. We could be talking to a lost ghost, a particular spirit guide, a relative of someone at the circle or a visiting spirit. A good process of elimination follows in the next few questions, which help to smoke out the true nature of the invisible visitor.

"No" another stern answer.

"Do you know where you are?" we asked.

"No" the table had tilted and knocked back to upright twice.

"Do you know why you are here?" A negative answer to this question is a sure sign of someone who is a bit lost and confused.

"No."

"Can we help you, friend?" Offering our services may melt the ice and find out if this visitor knew what he wanted or why he was here.

"No"

"Do you know that you are dead?" a million dollar, loaded question.

"No, I'm not."

"You are, friend. Why would you be speaking to us at a seance where we cannot even see you?"

"I don't approve of seances. I've come to stop you."

"Well if you don't approve of them, how come you are at one?" we asked another thought-inspiring question.

"I don't know."

At last our visitor had opened up a little and admitted he didn't really understand, so it seemed appropriate to take things further. We continued our information gathering.

"Who are you friend? I think we may be able to help solve a few mysteries for you."

"I'm a Priest, a man of God"

"Well God Bless You. You are a good man but probably a bit confused."

So, this explained a great deal. Death hadn't been all this man expected, not the big deal with Pearly Gates and strumming angels, so he didn't believe he had died at all.

"Yes, things are rather strange."

"You have passed over friend. Whilst things are strange they are ok and you will be all right. We can help you regain your bearings and help you on your way. Would you like to give it a try?"

"Yes I would, thank you." Our Priest was warming to us, gone was the stern disapproving manner.

We then encouraged the Priest to think of someone he loved who had died ahead of him and open his mind and look for that person beyond the physical boundaries of the room.

"Yes, I see them. Thank you. I'll go with them. God Bless You." The Priest's enthusiastic and joyful departure was another satisfactory rescue.

It amazes me sometimes that we can allow ourselves to have such fixed beliefs that we limit ourselves by them. We have ideas and beliefs about what our next life or spirit world is like. I've read loads of books about the nature of the spirit world and now simply conclude that even if I saw what it will be like, that idea would not fit in my head. Why try to hold such firm and restricting beliefs of what will be, when really what is of most concern is making what we are doing NOW work well for us all?

Each NOW is the most important moment of this life, we should perhaps concentrate more on getting this NOW right rather than working for the afterlife.

How sad to spend a whole life preaching of fixed images of God, Heaven and Hell only to find that you may have been mistaken. How can we possibly know exactly what life after this life will be like? Even if we could know what it's like, so what? What value is there in knowing, if we fail to get our act together here and NOW?

I don't wish to be too heavy about this as I totally respect the value of Religion and the strong community spirit and caring that it inspires. I would just love people to retain an open mind about the next dimension, for their own good. We each interpret each other's communication in our own way so why adopt a fixed belief when all ideas of the nature of after life are someone's personal interpretation?

However divinely the idea of after-life is inspired, it is still interpreted in many different ways when it is communicated to the masses. I do respect everyone's right to their own interpretation of what reality is and what the afterlife is but would love it if everyone could be just a little open-minded, especially when they pass over.

The Priest is one example of many people who came to the seance as confused ghosts, not believing in their own passing over because it just didn't fit into their narrow, expected reality.

Cossack rescue - an amusing physical manifestation

In one group, who joined me at a sitting for rescue work, there was a gifted medium Geoff, who was adept at allowing spirits to operate his body whilst he was in a state of consciousness rather than going into a state of trance. In other words he could let spirits operate his body movements whilst he was completely awake; it is more usual for such movements to occur when a medium is in a state of trance and therefore unconscious of the movements of his body.

Now, not wishing to be too frivolous about this but wanting to share an amusing rescue with you, I'll relate the story of the Cossack rescue.

We had been sitting a while and performed several rescues, we had conversed with the usual protecting or guiding spirits when Geoff, the medium, began to smile.

Now I wondered why Geoff was beginning to smile and in the same instant I knew. His lower body had begun to move from back to front and subtly from side to side at the same time, in a slow, peculiar rhythm.

No wonder Geoff was smiling, it looked so funny I was finding it difficult to control my laughter.

"God Bless You." I gave the standard greeting trying to get a grip on my humour.

So we regained our dignity and compassion, just. The conversation continued with Geoff still moving, sometimes speeding up the rhythm and at others slowing down. It transpired that this Ghost was a Russian Cossack, dead, but still believing he was riding the horse he so dearly loved.

One funny thing, was when Geoff started to ride the horse so violently that he laughed and said "Slow down for heavens sake". The Cossack did slow down and he listened to our advice. He accepted that being dead would explain why things had been so strange.

So he was rescued and off he went with his horse into the spirit world.

Geoff's ability to be so relaxed and trusting of temporary ghost's possession of his body, as seems to occur in some mediums, is really excellent.

Geoff is also very sensitive to presences and deals with it in a most natural and relaxed fashion. When he feels some ghost come close to him he'll simply say "Buzz off. Can't you see I'm busy? Come back later". No drama, no fuss, just as normal as dealing with any person, and why not treat ghosts as though they are normal? It's rather like the ongoing issue of sighted people treating the blind as though they are stupid or cannot speak for themselves.

Why not just understand the disability of not knowing they are dead? We can tell them with gentle love that they are dead and how they can find their relatives, simply by thinking of ones already passed over.

Group rescues

In the previous section we considered the idea of many ghosts watching whenever a relevant rescue is taking place, all crowding around to see what's going on. Almost as we mortals will crowd in the street to watch a dramatic, even tragic scene, fascinated by the emotion and drama.

Well, I reckon, as we're pretty similar when we 'pass over' it's quite reasonable to believe that we still enjoy the dramatic and have the same curiosity that we experience here.

The attraction for ghosts to watch events like seances and sittings has been described to me as though there is a huge light shining up from the earth into the sky, that spirits or ghosts are drawn to from far and wide.

You can imagine that once we are removed from so much of our day-to-day material sensations and distractions, our awareness of another plane would become greatly magnified. Just as the hearing of a blind person becomes so acute.

I liken the sensitivity of ghosts drawn in to a sitting to see what's going on, to the shark drawn into a frenzy of feeding fish, the shark knowing instinctively that there may be something for him there.

So, all these ghosts are drawn in - "Is there something for me here?" they wonder, as they watch one rescue and hear someone told that they've been dead all this time. They hear how the person's experience was of being shunned and feeling isolated from their friends and family for no apparent reason. They begin to think, "that's what it's been like for me" and the thought goes on to make them wonder if they are dead too.

All the old dogma of belief can limit them here. Such ideas as "but I don't believe in ghosts", "there is no afterlife", "seances are a load of rubbish and trickery" can limit the dead person's mental agility and make it harder for him to keep an open and aware mind. He'll keep trying to find an explanation he prefers, like the fellow earlier who justified being ignored by everyone by saying "they're all so stuck up round here, they won't even speak to a fellow any more".

Eventually, perhaps after being drawn to watch a few rescues or maybe at the first one, our subject tries the advice given for himself or he pushes to the front of the queue and says "me next" and comes into the sitting. Trying himself could simply be the process of repeating the exercise he's seen, and just thinking of his relatives who died already could serve to reunite him with them. The pushing and shoving of spirits trying to get through is hard to imagine. However if you think of a chance to speak to people for the first time after thirty or so years when you really need company and love, it becomes easier to appreciate the extent of the need.

Here the importance of the role of a spirit to act as a 'doorkeeper' can be better appreciated, someone has to hold back the rush of ghosts and spirits wanting to communicate with the people sitting at a seance. It is the doorkeeper who does just that, he decides who will speak and lets one through at a time. From my experience doorkeepers are usually quite powerful and committed spirits who in their lives demonstrated their strength of purpose. There have been Masai warriors, Samurai swordsmen, Red Indian braves and chiefs, Roman soldiers. There would be no mistaking the bravery of such fearless people and the crowd of spirits equally get the message and await their turn.

In the state of being a ghost, one thing that I understand can happen is that similar people are drawn together. No surprise really because that is what happens here in our mortal lives, groups are formed of people sharing similar beliefs or having experiences in common. So ghosts attract each other in the same way. They don't always know about each other's presence, they may not believe in ghosts and will see nothing other than the material world.

Some however do see each other and go around together sharing their confusion and playing as best they can. One such group that I saw rescued was a group of young children. I don't believe they died together but as children they formed almost a spiritual play group and whilst they missed their parents and did not understand what was going on; they played and laughed together between their sad and lonely moments.

It was terribly sad at the seance when the first child of the group 'came through'. We all love children and want them to be joyful and feel so loved, that it really was pretty distressing to sense such a sad little presence. The child was a typical case really, didn't know where it was, why had its parents gone all funny?

The child was asking all the questions you'd expect from a child that didn't know he was dead. Fortunately, having had little indoctrination in his short life, the child quickly accepted his new state of being and instantly agreed to think of its Granny. Off the child went with his relative into the 'spirit world'.

Having seen their playmate safely talk to the strange group of adults all the other children watching wanted some of the same. One by one they rushed through. It was incredible for me to experience, we didn't really need to be there at all, these kids had really got the message. They'd rush in. They'd say a quick "God Bless You", our standard greeting to spirits, and almost immediately say "Yes I see her", as they rushed off into the spiritual arms of their waiting relative.

This is one of the most joyful experiences I have ever had; it really is amazing to experience the relief and joy of around twenty kids all discovering that they are still loved after all. It was like hundreds of orphans being met off a train by their parents, it was absolutely mind-blowing.

So group rescues are like that. There have been similar ones with soldiers all from the same battle or platoon. The first ghost comes through and learns that he has died, then they quite often all go at once without bothering to 'come through' the sitting individually.

We've rescued whole military groups from German submarines who died in battle and were not rescued until the 1980's. To me that's the real tragedy of war. Not the loss of life but how long the suffering of confused death goes on. There are people still fighting wars today where they died, often fighting ghost after ghost.

The friends I sat with, Tony and Patricia, still do amazing rescue work in their current lives and they are happy for me to share this with you. They have been working for themselves on the south coast and have found the most practical way to take a break is to pop over to France for long weekends rather than leave the business for too long. This has led to the evolution of group rescues involving soldiers from the World Wars.

Tony and Patricia have found that more and more military types are coming for rescue through their circle. When rescued, these spirits often ask my friends to visit certain war graves or battle fields to rescue the rest of the brigade or company.

One spirit came through and this is a transcript of his experience as he describes it. He specifically asked that his story be included in this book, in full.

The brackets like this ( ) are his, and the ones like this { } are those of the couple who had the experience and who comment at the end of the spirit's story, which they transcribed at a seance.

Peter's Story
– transcribed through a medium, Patricia, in 1991

"I came to visit the circle of those who have become my friends, giving only the name 'P'. To whet their appetites I gave them information slowly one piece at a time, like a jigsaw puzzle. I told them I was German, that I fell in the war along with many of my comrades. I told them that I was buried near Abbeville, conveying the impression, deliberately, that I fell in the first great conflict. I told them that a tree was of great significance, therefore adding to the mystery. I told them my second initial 'H'.

A holiday had already been put into their minds – to visit again (they go frequently) to the battlefields of Northern France where so many of those who fell {ghosts}, are fighting to this very day. I visited them at each of their small meetings and agreed to travel with them.

A plan was agreed between them, that they would visit as many cemeteries as possible looking for what they thought was a needle in a haystack.

On departure day, they left early full of enthusiasm for the task ahead. On the way to their destination they (we) visited several burial plots and scanned the stones therein for Germanic graves tucked into corners of sacred ground. For those of you not aware of the fact, the burial consortium {War Graves Commission} is very good to its enemies. They tend our graves as well as their own. We the enemy, are buried, in some instances, where we fell. So we occupy in death, the ground that we all fought for in life.

The holiday was not to be a long one so time was pressing. In their quest for my burial plot they visited many large and many small cemeteries. Some of these have no visitors and are largely forgotten. A prayer was said in each, quietly. Thoughts for the fallen were expressed, many people were helped.

Eventually, as the holiday neared its end, a German cemetery, tucked away (large German cemeteries are hidden from general view) in a wood down a long winding road was spotted.

They knew that this had to be the place where 'P.H.' lay with his comrades. We entered the chapel if that is what it can be called, through an imposing bronze door. The circular room is dominated by a weeping Madonna, several feet high. Out through another door and into the cemetery. They stood in awe. Over 22,000 comrades lie here, they appear to go on forever. They thought it was impossible except by luck, to find my stone. Finally Mrs A gave herself up to my directions and I led her directly to my stone. By my stone is a very distinctive tree, it has grown as three trunks from one seed.

I don't think they doubted that they would find my stone, but they were surprised when they did. We 3 stood and prayed for the salvation of my friends, that they should no longer fight the battle they had fought for so long. We prayed for peace, for comfort and for cleansing of the Spirit. Now it is their turn to speak......................

Tony and Patricia's account.

"Our friends name is Peter H. he served in the German army and was killed in 1940 aged 28, his grave is near Abbeville, we surmise that he was killed on the Abbeville. The cemetery is as he describes it. It was a cold, cheerless place, a cold that has nothing to do with the weather. We have photos of all this.

"We have been back to his grave since and placed a Remembrance Day cross there with kind, healing words written on the reverse.

"At a subsequent circle we were told "The cross has kindled a flame that will burn into eternity. It will guide those who are wandering {your proverbial ghosts} towards a greater understanding of their circumstances and they will then get help."

"On our second visit the cemetery had a different atmosphere. The difference was so great that the whole place had come alive. Gone was the sadness of death, there was a celebration of life."

Note: At a circle, Peter specifically asked that the text he dictated be included in full in this book! I thank him for sharing his experience and hope that it is an inspiration to all who read it. I hope it also encourages peace and resolution of conflict by negotiation, rather than the sword.

Through their work, these friends of mine, Tony and Patricia, are helping to solve the problems created through the First and Second World Wars, which are simply not acknowledged by our society. It hardly needs to be said that they perform their rescues with no discrimination between nation, race or religion.

The search for Peter's grave

The tree with three trunks

Lance in the graveyard

Peter's grave

Eight

EXORCISM

An example of exorcism

Sometimes, these ghosts who wander lost and alone, become attracted to receptive or vulnerable people and hang around them. Some become so close that they somehow, get drawn into the 'aura', the magnetic or psychic field of that individual. It seems that once that happens, the ghost can find it hard to get away and can become convinced that he is in charge of the body he was following.

He may believe the body is his own and take control of it as best he can. This is a short view of how Spirit possession can occur.

There will be further comment on this subject later in the book, but first, here is an example of an exorcism of possessing ghosts.

My group was contacted by a woman who wanted help for her husband. The man, Robert, had been becoming really obsessive about washing his hands and had been taking on some strange mannerisms and habits. The couple, having moved to a new area two years before, had integrated well but Robert, previously a sociable man, had not made a single friend and loathed going out or meeting people. He seemed to want to keep himself to himself, which was quite out of character with his usual behaviour.

We agreed to see if we could help and raised the subject at our usual Monday night circle. The spirit people agreed that we would be able to help Robert who was, they said, possessed by ghosts.

Knowing we had the guidance of our band of Spirit helpers, we agreed to help. We arranged an appointment and travelled to the couple's home where we established our circle with the Lord's Prayer and a specific prayer for protection and to help Robert.

After the opening greetings from our usual guides, Patricia went into a trance and allowed a ghost to communicate through her.

This was the spirit of a man who had been horribly disfigured and had such an ugly face that he had been cruelly mocked by children and treated as an outcast. He thought he was still alive and still had the same ugly face. He thought that Robert's own body was his. Eventually we convinced him he had passed over, that was why he was speaking to us through a woman's body. When he opened his eyes to the spiritual dimension he saw that the room had become full of spirit children all dancing and singing asking him to come and play with them.

How could he resist such an offer after years of being ignored? And off he went.

It transpired that Robert had been home to five ghosts, of which our disfigured friend had been just one, but very significant in affecting Robert's behaviour.

You could understand how, with such a supposedly ugly presence inside him, Robert would get up and wash his hands then come back into his lounge, feel he was still dirty and go instantly to wash his hands again. How could he want to mix in social circles if he inherited the fear of revulsion felt by the spirit possessing him? No wonder he hadn't integrated into the neighbourhood.

Robert's possessing spirits were exorcised, but when we returned to our regular Monday seance we were advised that probably Robert would get possessed again as he hadn't really minded the presences and hadn't learnt how to protect himself from wandering souls. He could easily choose not to become possessed if he acknowledged and changed his willingness to be possessed.

An interesting point here, is that as our disfigured friend was so used to being ignored or shunned in his earthly life it would not seem unusual to him that once dead, people ignored him. This would make it even harder for him to work out what was going on. It could have been such a relief to him that the taunting had ended that he may have preferred being a ghost to being alive with such a deformed body. In fact, he enjoyed the company of the other ghosts who were also possessing Robert because they accepted him and didn't tease him about his appearance.

Self-exorcism and being followed around

In the section on the soldier brothers, who arranged to meet after the war, we looked at how the spirit of the soldier had heard the conversation I had with Alice and Paul. He had liked what he had heard, thought it made sense and as a result he had followed me around and attended the next seance.

Accept that the soldier could listen and follow me around, and you'll appreciate how I believe that whenever we talk of things relevant to ghosts or spirits then some of them will be listening.

I've had many conversations where the subject of ghosts has been brought up, usually by others, as I have only really come into the open about my beliefs since 1989. Often when the subject is broached I recognise that there are no accidents or coincidences and that the subject has come up for a reason. So, I'll simply state my view that Ghosts often don't know they're dead, they don't really understand why they cannot be seen and even if they did, they don't know what to do about it.

You can bet your life that if these things are said and a ghost is listening he'll be all ears! Then I go on to describe the simple process that a ghost can use to meet his relatives who have already died. You know, where they just think of their relatives and look beyond the dimension of the room. Exactly the same process as used in a rescue and if a ghost is listening, he may well try the process and rescue himself.

Just by having had the conversation, I feel a rescue may have taken place. As ghosts are attracted to listen it is quite important to describe the rescue process to give them a chance to try it rather than following me around to hear more.

Having tea, late one evening in Holland Park, London, I was drawn into a conversation on ghosts but did not quite take it all the way to the fruitful conversation described above. We chatted about ghosts but I was not able to get to a point where I could describe the rescue process.

I had not been drinking alcohol (you'll see why I mention this in a minute) and I drove back to Hertfordshire.

When I got into my car and began driving home I developed a terrible headache. Now I do not get headaches unless I poison my body with an excess of alcohol. I knew that this headache was not my own, because I simply do not get them.

I guessed that whoever was hanging round the house at Holland Park had followed me home and this is one sure way of getting my attention. Anyone who causes me pain, I do not ignore!

As I drove home, I simply said to the ghost causing the pain,

"Go away and I'll talk to you later. You're causing me pain and I don't need it, now that I know you're there. I'll talk to you when I get home."

The pain then eased and I continued my journey home.

To deal with the intruding spirit I simply sat down on my sofa, said The Lord's Prayer quietly and said a brief prayer to my Spirit Guides for protection and guidance. I used the same format as I would for a group of people sitting at a seance together, I wasn't scared as I recognise that ghosts do not want to harm anyone. They are naturally good just as we, and all living things, are innately good.

Then, having created a safe space for communication:

"God Bless you Friend. I know you're here because I felt you hurt my head. I imagine you may have been injured on the head at some time. Perhaps you died when your head got damaged. Anyway, thanks for listening and being here. You have passed over, out of your body and are now dead. This is good as it means that your head need not hurt any longer and you can get on with a life in the spirit world."

I paused to rest me, and to give the idea time to sink in.

"You are safe my friend. There is another world waiting for you. You don't have to hang around here all the time. To find that other world, all you have to do, is think of a loved one or relative who died before you. Think of them and then look for them, look beyond the room and you'll surely see them."

"Try it, and go in peace. If it doesn't work for you, come back another time, when you're ready to try again. God Bless You."

My headache never returned once I had agreed to speak to the ghost later. I feel that it was really vital that I kept my agreement with the ghost though. I expect my head would have hurt quite a bit more if I hadn't sat down and spent time talking to the ghost. I've never tested this by breaking such an agreement with a ghost and I do not intend to.

This process cured my headache and it rescued the lost spirit.

The satisfactory rescue was confirmed when I next sat at a seance. A regular spirit guide, whose opinion I really value, confirmed that there had been someone there who had caused the pain in my head. What's more the guide confirmed another successful rescue. The ghost had successfully made his way to the Spirit World by using the rescue process.

Just through the conversation I'd removed a ghost from a house in Holland Park and performed a rescue, I was delighted with the outcome.

In therapy for mortal people, there is a technique called 'secret therapy', this is where a technique is used to solve a persons problem without the therapist needing to know what the problem was. I feel that this form of ghost therapy is like that, a sort of 'secret ghost therapy' as it was successful without me ever hearing the ghosts opinion or his confirmation that he was willing or able to move on.

Now if I get pains for no apparent reason I look around to see if I can tell who's hurting.

Nine

AT HOME WITH SPIRIT

A child sees a ghost

Children are often recognised as being more open to their clairvoyance than adults. When children have a playmate who is invisible to their parents, I suspect they have a spirit companion. We seem to outgrow our psychicness and our western society seems to help us focus on the material factors of our environment rather than developing a spiritual awareness.

Just as some people attribute animals as having a greater psychic vision than humans, so I believe the uncorrupted perception of a child can be greater in some respects than an adult's.

An example of this natural extra perception is demonstrated by the experiences of Tony and Patricia and their youngest daughter, Sally.

They also show how the whole family take the spiritual side of life completely in their stride, it's as normal as you or I going to the Post Office. I'll give you just a couple of examples of this now.

When Sally was 4 years old she was playing in the hall of the family's Victorian house. Her elder sister was at school full time so Sally was playing on her own.

She was sitting at the foot of the stairs with a toy car, pushing it to the front door then following to retrieve it, where upon she'd sit by the front door and launch it towards the stairs and the whole process would be repeated. You know how kids are, this was going on for a while and the child's mother got quite used to the sound of the car hitting the front door followed by the scampering and delighted giggles of her daughter.

Suddenly the noise stopped. Doesn't sound end abruptly sometimes? The silence was deafening and caught the mother's attention immediately. Sally's mother came to the foot of the stairs from the breakfast room to see her daughter sitting there apparently ok, but looking up at the front door.

"Who's that man mummy?" The child asked.

The mother, seeing nothing but accepting that there was someone there who her daughter could see, simply said "No one to worry you dear".

Addressing the ghostly visitor she said "Please could you go away, can't you see you're frightening my daughter?"

The child carried on playing as before, she was happy to retrieve her car from the foot of the door, now that the stranger had gone.

At their next circle the visitor 'came through' and apologised for his intrusion. He explained that he had lived at the house and was simply a soldier back from the war looking for his parents, he hadn't meant to startle anyone.

The soldier quickly grasped the point when he was told he must be dead and that it was 1969 and he willingly thought of his parents and went off to the world of spirit with them.

The next example occurred when Sally was a little older. She was woken in the night to find her supposedly dead Auntie standing in her bedroom. "What are you doing here Auntie?" The child asked, completely relaxed about the whole business.

"I want to be in Bournemouth with Edith, and I don't know how to get there dear." The Aunt replied.

"Just think you're there and you will be, Auntie." The child so wisely answered. Instantly the Aunt was gone.

It seems that spirits travel so easily once they are aware that they are not limited by time or space. They really do only have to think of someone or somewhere and they are there. Until they know that they are dead however, they have to wait for buses or get a lift. Can you imagine how long it would take a ghost to hitchhike?

It's great to meet a family where ghosts of Auntie, Rescues and Spiritual Healing are just a way of life. To them it's simply the way it is. They live their lives totally in accordance with their morals, love their neighbours and have rescue circles to help as much as they can.

A spiritualist's guide to car buying

Tony and Patricia are totally committed to a Spiritual way of life, doing all they can to help with their rescue work and still enjoying their own lives. They follow the guidance they are given and this can cause some interesting situations; like the time Tony was given advice on changing his car.

Tony was told that it was time to change his car by a Spirit Guide. Now Tony liked his car, it was one which his Spirit Guide helped him find and recommended.

"But I don't want to change my car." Tony told his Spirit Guide.

"We've lined up another car for you, and besides, we've got someone waiting for yours." This was a clear message from Tony's guides for him to look out for another car.

I think they told him the make and colour of his new car and that he would "just see it" and know it was the one. Sure enough, Tony saw exactly the car, so prominently displayed that he knew it must be the one.

Interesting though, that when a Spirit Guide considers the life of his charge he also knows the importance of considering the effect of that life experience on others. Respecting how our lives are all intertwined must be incredibly complex.

Seeing how hard some people find life here, I reckon we should consider ourselves lucky that we don't have the responsibility of being spirit guides. That must be a really tough job. Imagine the negotiations that must take place when ten people go for the same job. I can almost picture twenty or thirty Spirit Guides all discussing the merits of their candidate and the spirits' debate could even include the spirit guides of each applicant's present employer who wants to keep his existing staff at all cost.

It's an amazing image and one too complex for my head. I just enjoy what I can understand, who needs answers to situations like that? Mind you, if anyone did unravel that picture I'd love to read about it.

Ten

HAUNTINGS

Haunting is just an easy rescue

Since I began sharing my beliefs, openly, with my friends, I have been asked for advice on hauntings. An example follows where to the inexperienced, things could have seemed quite frightening, with banging sounds coming from an empty house, interference with a record and cassette player plus the breaking of a wine glass. As you'll see, it was all within the usual pattern and not dangerous at all.

My friend Michele phoned me one day.

"Lance, I don't know how to put this but I think my house is being haunted."

We had a conversation about the goings on at her 1950's semi in a Hertfordshire New Town. Here is Michele's description of the goings on:

The first thing that happened was on a few occasions I would find various lights on (in the bathroom, bedroom and lounge) when I knew that I had not left them on.

Nothing too spooky I thought.

Then I was woken from a deep sleep one night by a lot of banging sounds. It actually sounded as though someone was banging on the lounge door, directly beneath my bedroom door. The dog had run upstairs and was sitting at the bottom of my bed looking pretty disturbed. (At this time he was only a few months old and was not into barking or sounding aggressive).

I got up and went downstairs and found nothing. Went back to bed and started to drift off to sleep, with the dog settled at the bottom of the bed, when more loud banging sounds made us both jump up. We sat for a while then I went downstairs again – even went outside to see if it was something in the garden. Nothing. Back to bed and after a while, drifted off to sleep. All quiet.

The following day I asked the neighbours if they had heard anything and they said that they had heard noises from my house and that sometimes they heard quite a lot of noises when I wasn't in the house.

The next episode was the video recorder. I was busy cleaning upstairs and when I came downstairs the video was recording some programme. I had not pre-set it to tape anything!

Then one weekend a friend, (call her) Julie, came to stay. On the Saturday evening we had been watching T.V. and drinking some wine and chatting about a number of things, one of them being the subject of ghosts and spooks.

At the end of the evening I went upstairs to the bathroom and retired to my bedroom. Julie used the bathroom after me and went back downstairs to sleep on the sofa bed, which I had made up for her. On her return to the lounge I heard an almighty scream and came running downstairs. Only to find that the wine glass she had been using, and had placed on the coffee table before using the bathroom, was now lying in shattered pieces all over the bed which she was just about to sit on!

The last thing to happen was about 2 months ago when I came home one evening with my boyfriend Robert and I decided to play some music.

I switched the Hi-Fi system on and placed a cassette into the deck and pressed the play control. As I moved away from the system the volume went crazy and suddenly we were deafened by the music. I quickly switched it down and began to walk away again and the same thing happened again.

Must be the cassette deck being faulty I thought. So I switched everything off and then began again by playing a record. Just as I was about to move my boyfriend said "O.K. so if there is someone there, do it again." within seconds we were deafened by the music.

We both felt spooked and he checked all the wiring etc. Then he decided to put something on. Put a record on and everything seemed fine. He looked at me and I said "Don't say a word". He looked at me and started to laugh and with that the music went up to the highest volume. He jumped and quickly switched it down. I told him to switch it off and we left the room.

Michele described all this and I agreed to come round in a week or so when we were both free. She wasn't panicking about the goings on at her house, so there was no rush.

I told her that I would deal with the ghost and if anything else happened in the meantime, it would be ok to tell the ghost to stop and wait until I came round to talk to it next week.

I arranged that Michele and I would sit and chat to the ghost then go out for dinner so we could leave the house empty to see if anything happened.

Michele greeted me warmly and we went into the lounge and chatted. I looked briefly at the video and the Hi-Fi, then we sat and relaxed. As I am not consciously Clairvoyant or Clairaudient I was not going to attempt to hear the ghost answer me or ask any questions that required an answer.

Having seen so many rescues and recognised a pattern that always worked, I was willing to simply address this ghost and assume it would listen and understand.

We began with The Lord's Prayer and then I said a short prayer to my own spirit guides asking for protection and help for Michele and me, in our effort to help the confused spirit.

Then I began to speak to the ghost and I'll set out as well as I can recall what I said.

"Hello friend. Thanks for coming to listen to what I will say to you. I cannot actually see you or hear you, but you have helped us know that you are here by the things you have done to attract attention. I've heard about the banging when you are left on your own during the day and the volume control on the stereo that you love to play with. I've heard about the broken glass.

"I understand that you are confused and you just want to be acknowledged. Well God Bless You friend, we love you and care about you. That's why we are talking to you, because we love you and we can help you.

"You know how you have been thinking that things are a bit strange? You have been ignored by people for some time. You are feeling lonely. Well that's because you died my friend. You have passed out of your body and that's why I can't see you and why so many people seem to have ignored you. They just didn't know that you were there."

"It's ok though, you are perfectly safe. I suggest you could be in a much better place than hanging around Michele's house all day on your own. You can be with your loved ones. family you love, who have died before you, are waiting for you. You can be with them easily, now.

"All you need to do, is think of them and look around you, beyond the room you are in and you'll see them. I hope you're willing to give that a try. We love you and want to help you. Try thinking of them and if you see them then go safely with them. If it doesn't work, remember that we love you, want to help and you can be here while you try again to understand what's going on."

"Please think of your loved ones and go with them. God Bless You Friend."

I said a quick prayer to thank my Guides for their support and protection and also to wish our friend well, then we went out for our dinner.

I didn't tell Michele but I was wondering if the house would be a bit disrupted when we got back if the spirit hadn't gone. All was well however and Michele has heard no more from her neighbour of the banging and no more broken glass.

Michele's comment: "Since then nothing out of the normal has happened."

The importance of this episode for me is that I had performed a Rescue without a medium present. This was a clear demonstration to me that any one of us can Rescue lost souls if we use that same formula and understand that a ghost is just a confused dead person. A ghost has no interest in doing harm and just wishes to be acknowledged, included and helped to find its friends.

My objective in writing this book as I said earlier is to help prevent anyone being so confused, when they die, that they become a ghost. Perhaps now I should add that I'd like us all to be able to help Ghosts 'over' to the spirit world.

Eleven

RESCUE WORK – PROBLEMS & COMPLICATIONS

Having introduced and covered some examples of rescues to demonstrate the idea, you are now familiar with the concept of convincing a ghost that he's dead and how to help him find the family and friends he can be united with on the 'other side'.

The next area to explore is other rescues where things didn't go in the same straightforward pattern or they demonstrate some other idea about the experience of death and passing on.

The following examples were obtained during the 1990's using the same simple method of communicating with 'spirits' as was described earlier; that is using a table, which taps for yes and no and can spell out words to confirm the ideas obtained as a medium would obtain them.

Non – religious people

On some occasions when the table moves for yes and we at the seance or circle, greet the new invisible visitor with our customary "God Bless You", we get two taps of the table for "NO". This indicates to us that the Ghost has no real belief in a God and is probably lost and may have been unable to acknowledge his own death.

In these circumstances we chat to the ghost about the confusing experiences that we know he's been having. From our work we know that the ghost will almost certainly have tried to speak to mortal people, who will have ignored him. This will have been very confusing and upsetting, especially if the people who wouldn't speak to the ghost were his own family and friends.

We ask if the ghost can remember when he last had a meal and how he explains having come into the room without opening the door.

Through these conversational questions we often develop trust and rapport, showing an understanding of the ghosts own dilemma.

On the religious aspect, it really seems simple enough. If you believe that there is no after-life, if you have any feeling of 'being', you cannot be dead. This fixed belief in the absence of a God and heaven causes this ghost to be convinced that he's as alive as you are and this can make the rescue quite time consuming.

To convince someone like this of an after-life takes considerable skill, patience and experience. I have to be sensitive to the person's suffering and often, their sadness. They often get the feeling, "How can there be a God if he lets me be so badly treated and ignored?"

Once the ghost is open to the idea that he has died, things accelerate apace. If you suddenly found a possible solution to a cause of deep sadness, you'd be keen to explore the possibilities too.

Sometimes it is necessary to suggest that if they believe that there is nowhere else, no heaven or spirit world, they have nothing to loose by going to see it. This then opens their mind to the idea of having a look and we get them to do the same exercise for most rescues.

Religious types

The people who die with a strong and fixed religious view are sometimes visitors to our rescue circle. Unfortunately a very rigid expectation of what you'll see when you die can cause an inability to accept that death has taken place. Perhaps you can imagine a person who has followed a religion with determination all their lives, saying "When I die, I am going to be with God. I've worked hard for Him and been a good person, I'll go straight to Heaven when I die. I haven't seen St Peter at the Gates, so I know I'm alive. Anyway, I don't approve of seances."

We then spend time showing our compassion for the confusing experiences the person has been having, although these are sometimes justified by the ghost by blaming the other people who have been ignoring him.

"They are just sinners, they know that I am a holy person and far too good for them to speak to."

Eventually, we always build a rapport and convince our ghostly visitor of his condition of having died. After that it's again very easy to get him to open his eyes in a new way to the spirit world.

The example earlier in the book of the Priest who disapproved of seances is exactly the sort of rescue that occurs with some devout religious people. I am not saying that religion is wrong or does any harm, I am simply suggesting that there is great value in having an open mind. All religion is surely the best interpretation that we mortals can understand and is a belief, not a fact. Even my own philosophy, where information can be obtained from 'the other side' remains unproven and simply a belief.

Blind people

Recently at a rescue circle, we had a ghost come through and we easily convinced him that he had died and we began the exercise of encouraging him to think of friends and relatives who had died previously, with whom he'd like to be re-united.

This exercise includes the idea of the ghost filling his heart with memories of the people he'd like to see again and when he is filled with joy and love for them, we say

"Now spring open your eyes and look beyond the room."

At that point the ghosts invariably see their old friends in the distance, gradually coming towards them to take them into the spirit world.

With this particular ghost, we found that he had no success at the rescue process and eventually the most perceptive or mediumistic person perceived that this person may have been blind before death.

On asking the ghost if he was blind, we got a "yes" and were able to progress using the sounds of his friends' voices and laughter.

The ghost moved on to the spirit world, where he no longer would have the physical disability of blindness.

A retarded person's ghost

During one rescue circle, where we were attempting to explain that a ghost was no longer alive, with a physical body, we seemed to be making no progress. Naturally, with so many successful rescues and a formula that worked so well we wondered what the difficulty was.

After a while it finally dawned on us, or to the most psychic person at the seance, that the man, now a ghost, had been mentally retarded and was finding our conversation as confusing as his experience and it wasn't helping him at all. In the light of this realisation we acknowledged his condition and rebuilt rapport, showing that there really was no need for him to try to understand and that as he no longer had a physical body, his thoughts didn't need to remain restricted by his old physical condition.

Amazingly, the suggestion worked and the ghost took on a new level of communication and quickly grasped the point and the rescue process succeeded in getting him to the comfort of his old friends and family in the spirit world.

Children

Another interesting and rewarding group of people to rescue have been children. Often they are just sad that their parents have ignored them and they don't understand, but they can still be jolly. Children are pretty used to not understanding and this together with their resilience enables them to keep their spiritual chins up.

It's good when the ghost of a child accepts that its parents really do love it, they just thought that the child was dead. Children find the discovery that they're dead such a relief "So they really do love me?". Being dead is easier for them than being unloved, after all they are used to learning new things and a new spirit world is just another exciting new adventure.

An amusing rescue with a child was when telling a child that I understood his condition and his confusion, the child retorted,

"Of course you do, you're a grown up." The little ghost didn't really expect to understand his own position.

When attempting the rescue exercise with a child, there have been times when there has been no relative or friend that the child has known who could have been in the spirit world. No relative has already died, to his knowledge, so he had nobody to think of when looking for spirits to lead him to the other world.

In these cases, we get the children to 'play pretend' and ask them to imagine a game they would like to play with other children. Then to imagine seeing that game being played and hear the sounds of children laughing and other sounds associated with the game. When that picture is vivid the ghost child is encouraged to spring open its eyes and look beyond the room. In every case, so far, the child sees other spirit children and goes to join the game in the spirit world.

This versatility in approaching ghosts is very important and the use of some method for communication and to get confirmation of their understanding can be very important.

One amusing thing that happens quite often with ghosts of children is that they hang out in big groups. There have been times when we've rescued one child and others turn up saying "And me" demanding, as only children can, not to be left out or forgotten. Then they all go to the other side together.

Orphans

There have been ghosts of orphan children who have felt bitter towards the world and have not believed that there is any better place than the confusing world of an earthbound or lost spirit. Often these children seem to meet up and gather together and play in the earth sphere. These children often need a fair bit of encouragement to move on. Sometimes, whilst a bit lonely, they are making the most of their situation and can be responsible for quite a few hauntings, where things move about the house.

I suppose compared with the lonely life of hardship being a street urchin, hungry and poor, being a ghost isn't so bad. It is a shame for these characters to accept such a boring life, doing hauntings, when with a little extra effort they can be developing and being loved in the world of spirit.

With orphans it is obviously difficult to get them to think of relatives that they want to see who have died. They don't know who their parents were, or even if they were dead, if they'd want to see them ever again after abandoning them.

In these cases, we encourage the orphan to think of a friend who had died, or to play pretend as just described in the section on child rescues.

Convicts and sinners

Even when you realise that you've died, if you have led a very sinful life and even committed murder, what would you expect to happen?

In our culture, we might expect that sinner to go to Hell when he dies. So if you were a sinful person, what would you do?

You'd hide! You'd be afraid of being found and would accept any sort of 'earthbound' existence rather than being found and condemned to the burning pits of Hell for all eternity.

Just like the child at a grown-up's party, he'd rather be bored on his own hiding behind a settee rather than be found and sent to bed!

There have been many rescues of convicts and people who have led quite wicked lives. In one rescue a whole load of convicts had been hanging out, hiding, together in a prison. Clever really, nobody would think of looking there and they know the system in prison.

So how do we convince the convicts to come out of hiding?

As always, rapport is built, through an understanding of their fears and experience, then we suggest an alternative. We suggest that the world is not about Hell and damnation, but about learning and love. We suggest that rather than hiding for ever, would it not be better and more constructive to go and see the people they wronged (if they are dead already) and attempt to put right what they did to hurt them. I also suggest that surely the people who had been wronged would have a new understanding of the sinner in that spirit world.

Surely the sinner would have the chance to put right what he'd done? Is this what karma is? The chance to see the result of our actions, reaping what we sow.

In any event, the hiding sinners willingly accept the challenge to move into a new dimension of life. So, in their case, often they know they're dead, but they are just trying to avoid Hell. Well the fact is, you can die but you can't hide forever from your actions.

Reuniting with a loved one

After death, a lovely lady was aware that she had died but was hesitant about moving to the spirit dimension. She was not afraid of being judged for she was a good person who was much loved by everyone who met her, including me.

She was hesitant for she had outlived her husband by many years, as women often do, and she was worried that she would be old and unattractive to her husband who died at his prime. She as a spirit asked a psychic friend for guidance and was reassured that she would be welcomed and beautiful to him and she moved to that other place.

When we die we take on the form that we were most comfortable with, our back aches, rheumatism, arthritis are all put behind us as we express ourselves in the spiritual representation of our best image.

Often I've heard of widows seeing the spirit of their husband and saying how handsome and tall he stood, as he did when he was younger or before he fell ill.

A chap the other day saw a recently deceased relative that he was no longer deaf, that now he was free of his body, he could hear perfectly.

People are fitter and healthy after death and take on the best representation of themselves.

So any worries about meeting loved ones, be assured that you will be seen through the eyes of love and as you were in the most perfect moment of your love.

Twelve

MORE RESCUE WORK – HAUNTINGS

An office with a ghost

In addition to being called to people's homes when they are haunted, I have been asked to help remove ghostly presences from offices.

Here is an example of an office which was haunted, the case is written up in the form of a brief report, the sort sent to the client following the rescue.

This example is also useful as it shows just how crowded with ghosts a haunted building can be but there can still be ghosts there who think that they are totally alone – they do not see the other ghosts.

The building:

Built in 1868 next to a church for use as a Manse. One of the oldest remaining buildings in the town. Now used as offices on both floors.

Occurrences:

Several sightings of a woman's ghost in floral dress by various staff members, over the years. Often people seeing this lady would assume that she was really there, but on looking again she would be gone. Searches were made of the building but to no avail, and nobody else would be wearing similar clothes who may have been mistaken for this lady.

A woman's ghost is often seen typing on an old fashioned 'Remington' manual typewriter.

Sounds of typing would be heard in reception area.

In one particular room was a 'bad feeling' experienced by one staff member in particular. He experienced very strong depressing feelings and found it difficult to work in that room.

Around seven people can be found who have offered reports of the sightings in the office of the woman.

At the office during the evening of 13/1/92:

The rescue team visited the building and walked around quietly, entering all the rooms.

All went well, we certainly agreed that one room seemed 'atmospheric'. I wondered if a previous resident was disappointed to see such a lovely room so sub-divided, but no evidence for this came forward during the later session.

We walked round the offices – just chatting to each other about what it would be like to hang around or be stuck in the office. What it would be like to have people working in what must have been such a lovely home. How upset I might be, for example, if that room had been mine, to see it divided. etc.

Then I said "Perhaps if I were stuck, I'd welcome the chance to chat to someone who could help. I'd drop round to see them, perhaps they'll do that later."

This conversation formed a sort of invitation to any curious spirits who had become bored with hanging around at the offices. An invitation to eavesdrop and then follow us for help. We closed all the internal doors, leaving the building as we found it and locked the front external door behind us. We went home to set up our Rescue Circle.

At home later that same evening:

We sat in our spirit circle, having begun with our prayers for protection and help for lost spirits. As we waited to start, I became deeply tired and sleepy, finding it hard to keep his eyes open.

"Wow, it's like having been asleep for years" I was wondering if I was picking up the energy of a tired ghost.

"Come on, wake up. This is like talking to Rip van Winkle, are you very tired?"

"Yes" came the ghostly answer, through the table.

The communication had begun, and through the slow process of communication through the table we established:

Nobody seemed to have any specific connection with the building we had visited, but all acknowledged that they had been hanging around there.

There were over twenty ghosts who had been hanging around together. We established that there were over twenty and less than 100, although we found some who may not have been included on the early count, as you'll read later.

The band of twenty plus, played and fooled around, teasing an older ghost called Norman, who may have been a Scottish farmer. I say may be, because while the ghosts still didn't realise their condition (ie having died) they were all communicating at once and some of the early evening messages were very confused.

We spoke with Norman and he became the spokesman for the group. Through Norman we encouraged them all to consider that they were dead – had lost their bodies. We tried to demonstrate how queer things were by reminding them of the motor car I had used (in case any had travelled with us), a vehicle without horses, and reminded them that they had entered the room and indeed the house, without opening any doors or travelling by horseback.

After some reassurance that the world could still be ok and that they still existed, they all accepted that they had died in the mortal sense. This seemed to explain their peculiar and confusing situation and why they hadn't gone out to get food etc. We asked, again through Norman, if they ALL had a friend or relative who had died, who they'd like to see again. When they ALL had identified a friend or relative – we proceeded with the exercise.

We got them to shut their eyes and recall the love for the person they wished to see, remembering the sound of their voice and laughter. When their hearts were filled with joy and love we asked them to 'spring open' their eyes and look beyond the room.

As they saw their friends and relatives they went off with them.

We invited any who wished to wait and give their names, to do so and one did, she said that she was:

Georgina Jameson – born 1863 in Eltham, which she started to spell as ELDHAM.

She had a 'given' or arranged marriage – not a happy one, she'd said and had moved to Hertfordshire. Her husband was Godfrey Pellant a jeweller from Berkhamsted.

One of our guides confirmed that this should be accurate and that "The building is now clear and all should notice the difference."

Then Beth sensed the presence of a farrier, as she had right at the beginning of the sitting, when we were identifying the Scottish farmer.

Our Spirit Guide simply said "Follow your instincts however peculiar."

Then the message, which subsequently we realised was from the farrier was, "Future in jeopardy, please help, lonely life, please help."

Now we knew that to a spirit who knows of the continuance of life beyond our mortal existence, the future can never be in jeopardy and we had never heard such a message from a guiding spirit. We knew this was another lost ghost.

With questioning we established that this was a farrier and he had also been at the office building, but had been unable to see the band of lost spirits playing their games and had been on his own. He had been ignored by the working staff at the office who he could see, so he felt even more lonely, ignored and confused.

He found it hard to accept that he had died, but eventually was persuaded that this was the only logical explanation. He then did the same exercise as the others and was reunited with his friends and family who having died came to meet him and introduce him to the spirit dimension.

Finally we had a woman come through, who may be named Rosie, who was quite disagreeable, in that she would not agree with anything we proposed to her for quite some time. She would not admit that things were strange for her and that she was confused by her presence in the room with us or why she was there. I suspect that the presence of this woman could have caused quite a bad environment should anyone be sensitive to her energy. She was, again after considerable effort, persuaded to accept her state and she admitted to being a bit scared, we reassured her that we had helped other people find their way to the spirit dimension and she agreed to do the exercise of seeking to attract her old friends. She had been successful in causing some misunderstanding during the early part of the sitting, but was able to realise her state and, like the others, went with her spirit friends.

We consider the rescue work on the office to be complete and trust that the distracted employee will find his office a more pleasant place to work.

It's interesting to reflect on the farrier who was in the same space but could not see over twenty other dead people in the office. He thought he was alone and ignored, therefore he was.

The session ended with a simple "Well done and good night" from our guiding spirit.

Comments from the occupants of the offices following the rescue

After meeting with the client, who called us in to sort out the office building, on Tuesday lunchtime (14/1/92) I learnt the following:

1– During the night of Monday, after leaving the offices, a framed year planner was knocked off the wall and some piles of files were knocked over.

2– The man who worked in the sub-divided office had been complaining of an overwhelming feeling of tiredness in his office, as I had when we sat.

3– Staff relations had been under additional strain.

From a conversation with the Local History Library at Blackheath I discovered that the town of Eltham has in fact had many names, none easily found in official records coincide with the one "ELDHAM", but this may have been in colloquial usage at the time.

Eltham has also been known by the following names at different times: Altham Doomsday Book, Healteham 1100, Aeltheham 1100, Helteham 1203, Elltham 1224, Ylteham 1270.

Regarding Georgina, it is not my intention to seek proof by researching her existence. In any event, where people have done such research and confirmed the accuracy of spirit readings, it doesn't serve as satisfactory proof.

The sceptics simply disregard the evidence saying such things as "the medium already knew the details", "unconsciously they are recalling the details from an obscure glimpse of an old electoral register", or even "it's just genetic memory – details passed on through generations in our genes". Sometimes they simply say it's made up or cheating.

The sceptics try so hard to ***not believe***, I think it's best to make their efforts easier by not offering such details.

For myself, I do not need proof. If the office is a nicer place to work and the staff stop seeing these ghosts, that's enough for me. It doesn't matter if it's true or not if an improvement is made. Personally, as you'd expect after considering this book, I do believe that the building was haunted and there is also a chance that Georgina did not give her real name. Two years later, before going to press, the staff still report an improvement to the atmoshere.

Patrick and others

I was contacted by a friend who knew of someone who was having ghostly experiences taking place in her home. I said that I was quite willing to go and visit the house and offered to stop the haunting.

The owner of the house had gone away for two weeks leaving the house empty. She returned to find that all the pictures hung on the walls had been moved and were no longer level.

Also the house was always cold, even when the gas central heating was on full blast, the gas fire in the lounge was needed in addition to the radiators to get the lounge warm.

We chatted about ghosts and how lonely and frustrating it can be being a ghost, and how easy it is to move on if someone shows you how. We noticed that the lounge was quite chilly at knee level and below.

On leaving the house we walked to my car, parked in the road outside the house, and found that the doors had been unlocked... a powerful spirit phenomena, as I always lock the car. Even visiting a haunted house wouldn't make me forget to lock the doors as haunted houses are not uncommon places for me to visit.

From the haunted house we drove to my home, fully expecting some or all of the ghosts to follow. As usual we knew that the ghosts would be curious to know more having listened to our conversation.

At home we opened the rescue circle in our usual way.

At the rescue circle

A small unsure little ghost came through who was from the house we'd visited earlier. This little person thought he was on his own and therefore the only ghost at the house. He'd only recently arrived there, although we didn't bother trying to establish what that meant in our time. He was happy to go and was reunited with his family from the Spirit World.

A group of three ghosts who had arrived at the house to hear our conversation about ghosts came through. They had not been haunting the house as they had only been there when we were there and left as we did. They grasped the idea that they were dead quite quickly and moved off to the Spirit dimension to meet their relatives.

Another child spirit came through and moved on to the Spirit World in the normal fashion.

We knew that there must be another ghost as none of these ghosts had been interested in moving the pictures as they had just been drifting around, not really conscious of where they were. Then another ghost made itself known through the table, tapping to say hello.

This ghost introduced himself as Patrick, a tricky street urchin a real 'survivor' type, with all the cunning and mischief of a street child of 100 years ago. Seen by the circle as a grubby child in shorts ending below the knee and lace up sturdy boots, this ghost acknowledged himself for his skill at moving the pictures. He also had been making the place cold.

In fact he also claimed responsibility for unlocking my car doors, when we'd left the haunted house. So he knew he was dead but didn't know where to go and was quite amused by moving things around. During our discussion he admitted that it did get a bit lonely and boring hanging around but he was used to surviving on his own, so it wasn't too bad for him.

After a long chat, Patrick seemed willing to take a look at the so called spirit world and we did the rescue exercise with him. He saw spirit children and went off he said, to join them in a game of marbles.

Later, Patrick came back to talk to us, pretending to be someone else, typical of his tricky mischievous manner. Fortunately we were not completely taken in and asked Patrick to stop messing around, which he did. Patrick explained that he didn't really think the spirit kids would take very kindly to him, as he'd had a hard life and had done some pretty bad things to survive his rough life.

After a while we almost convinced Patrick to go over to the other side, but he was still reluctant. We did succeed in persuading him to go up to the spirit children and ask if they would like him to join in with the game. Patrick did this and then reported back that he would be going....and off he went.

Patrick finally went and we closed the circle once one of our Spirit Guides confirmed that our rescue was complete. We had removed all the ghosts from the haunted house.

I then telephoned the owner of the house and said "Your house is all clear now. There were quite a few ghosts, but they've all gone."

"Are you sure?" she asked.

"Yes it's all clear." I replied, a little surprised at her question which I put down to normal nervousness about ghosts.

The next day, the friend who introduced me to the haunting and who was at the haunted house during my visit told me of the weird things he had experienced at the house after I had left the evening before. The central heating had gone haywire and the automatic valves on the radiators had taken on a will of their own.

I asked him to jot down what he'd noticed and his account follows:

"During the time Lance and his rescue team visited the property I was aware of a considerable chill in the living room despite sitting next to the radiator and with the fire on.

When a girl from the rescue team went to use the bathroom and generally check out the atmosphere upstairs, this chill eased but on her return a noticeable chill came back and remained even after they had left to go for their sitting.

After they had left, I went to the bathroom where I found the towel rail was, if not cold, at least cooled down to a level which would indicate that it had been off for some period of time.

A further check of the radiators in the house showed them all to be at the same, much reduced, temperature with the exception of the ones in the first and second bedrooms, which were not quite up to full temperature.

When we checked the boiler it was off, so we looked at the digital controller in the airing cupboard that was under a pile of laundry and could only be accessed by removing same. The controller was detached from its base and therefore not functioning. When it was refitted the system fired up again and the boiler functioned properly, it has to be said that the controller is not a good fit.

After a period of some twenty minutes I checked the radiators and found that whilst those in the bathroom and the three bedrooms were functioning normally, they were indeed too hot to touch, the radiators in the hall, dining room and living room remained cold.

The copper piping feeding the radiators was too hot to touch but the heat stopped at the thermostat taps. I detached each of the thermostat controls and the internal plungers were working freely with the valves set to open.

This was very odd, because the free movement of the valves suggests that the hot water should be able to flow into each of the radiators.

We cooked and ate dinner and as the temperature in the ground floor rooms remained low we drew the settee up to the open fire and I checked the radiators at periodic intervals but there was no change.

Approximately two hours after they left Lance telephoned to say that their sitting was finished and there had been more than one spirit presence at the house but these did not include the previous residents. Whilst he was on the telephone I again checked the radiator in the living room, which was about three feet from where I was sitting and this was too hot to touch as it subsequently proved were the other ground floor radiators. Those at first floor level had remained constant since the controller had been reconnected.

The temperature had risen to a comfortable level throughout the house and when I returned the following day, despite the fact that there had been no supplementary heating and only the central heating had been running, all rooms were at an acceptable level with the exception of the living room which I found to be uncomfortably hot." signed by my friend (9.2.92)

After reading my friend's description of his experience I understand why the owner asked for confirmation that the ghosts had gone. She saw the mysterious removal of the heating controller from its proper place, even though it was inaccessible due to the laundry, and the peculiar malfunction of the radiators as evidence that the ghosts may still have been there. It was only when I had rung to give the all clear, that the thermostatic valves had allowed the hot water to enter the radiators.

The story did not end their, however. My friend who introduced the haunting to me and who wrote the account above, gave me a ring.

"Lance, I think my house is haunted now!" We chatted about this and in our usual way, saw the humour in the idea that some ghost had moved in with him.

We discussed what had been happening in his house when he left it, with only his dog at home. This is a summary of the phenomena:

A grandfather clock, recently overhauled and usually reliable would stop ticking. Not only that, but the hands would move to different times, even to an earlier time before my friend went out and before the clock stopped.

Doors in the house would shut, locking his pet dog in the lounge. The door from the lounge into the kitchen has to be pulled shut from the lounge, something that his dog cannot do.

His house had also become terribly cold, very unusual because it was well heated and normally very warm.

To deal with this ghost I did as I normally do. I called round for coffee, set up a conversation about the boredom of hanging about in a strange house, not knowing how to move on and the like. We had the sort of conversation that is irresistible to a ghost. Once that was done, I popped back home and set up for a circle.

At the sitting the ghost from my chum's house came through. She confirmed that she had been at the previous haunted house, where Patrick's ghost had been. She was quite embarrassed at having followed the wrong person home, she realised her mistake and had tried to make her presence known to get further advice and help.

So she'd stopped the clock and almost waved the hands to attract attention, moving them to a different time to rule out a mechanical defect as a possible cause of the clock stopping. She had shut the doors, so that my friend would notice that things were different when he got in, things had been done that the dog could not do.

She hadn't wanted to be a nuisance, but had just wanted help. She had realised that she was dead, but needed to know how to move on, she went quickly to the Spirit World with our best wishes.

Of course, my friends clock is working well again and his house has warmed up. the dog can wander around the house happily when my friend goes out.

Car Window Operator

An attention seeking ghost was very successful in making its presence known by operating devices that were switched off.

This ghost turned out to be lost little girl who had died and was still seeking attention and this is how she got it.

When my friend parked her car and turned off the engine, the car stereo would come on, even though the power source was disconnected by the ignition switch! Once she had got out of the car and was standing near it with the car door open when the electric windows started to open on their own. There was no one in the car who could be operating the controls, apart from the ghost of the little girl.

The same child also performed an amazing feat by making a can of carbonated soft drink explode in a domestic refrigerator! The ring-pull had definitely not been used and the pressure to open the undamaged can had certainly been exerted from within the can. I took a similar can and placed it in my deep freezer and the same damage to the can occurred. Either my friends refrigerator was turned down to below freezing, a temperature which it cannot reach, or this child was able to reduce the temperature around the can to produce localised freezing. It is possible that the ghost was able to use some energy foreign to us to create the explosion of the drink from the can that made a terrible mess in the fridge.

Like all the lost spirits or ghosts I have encountered, this girl was glad of the opportunity to realise that she had died and move on to the comfort and love of her friends in the next dimension or spirit world.

Thinking of the living not the dead

Some rescues have been going well, with the ghost readily accepting his own death as an explanation for his difficulty in being heard by his living relatives, who didn't know he was there. Unfortunately after making good progress with this initial part, when we get to the rescue exercise, something seems to fail and the ghost is unable to see his friends from the spirit world. At first this was quite a shock to us rescuers, because the process always had worked. We were a perplexed until an inspired question of the ghost revealed that he had been thinking of his relatives still alive, in a mortal sense.

This meant that the relatives he was trying to see when he sprung his eyes open were the ones he'd just left when he died. Being mortally alive, of course the relatives were not visible in my lounge!

The relief at this discovery was immense and we began the rescue process again, making it even more clear that the ghost must think of people who are already dead, with whom he'd like to be reunited. Once this was established, the process was successful and the ghost moved on.

It's surprising how common this can be and how easy it is for those in a rescue circle to forget to check that the ghost will be seeking people from the correct dimension of being – already dead.

Knowing how to move on is crucial

One particular haunting amused me the other day. I went to tea with some friends and the subject of my work with ghosts and of this book came up.

"We've got a ghost" said the lady of the house. An all too familiar comment for me to hear by now.

I encouraged her to talk about her ghost. The lady told me that she often saw or sensed the ghostly presence of a woman, who was just there and didn't seem to do any harm.

"I often say to her *you can move on if you want to, you don't have to hang around here*" the lady continued with her story.

We chatted further and I said how frustrating and boring it can be to be a ghost and that part of my work is to help ghosts like theirs to move to the other side, to the spirit world.

I expected that the ghost would listen and be glad of the chance to hear some helpful information.

From all the times before, I knew that the ghost would be listening, eavesdropping, so I was expecting to hear from her next time I sat.

Sure enough, when we next sat at our rescue circle the ghost of the woman came through and said,

"I could hear the lady saying I could move on, but I didn't know how to do it." She also explained that it was quite nice there, the couple were very nice and they had some interesting visitors. We explained the rescue process and she chose to move on.

Just like the ghost who had been stopping the grandfather clock, she had realised that she was dead, but didn't know how to move on or where to go.

Thirteen

RESCUE WORK – SUMMARY

From the rescue examples above, you can see there are certain situations that can make the rescue a little more complex than was first apparent. There are many pitfalls in the process of 'ghost therapy' and I strongly suggest that this work only be undertaken by people who are able to build up experience through working with a sound rescue group.

Working with the advice and support of clear communication from Spirit Guides is important, so that a check can be made on the quality or completion of a rescue. The example of the ghost who followed the wrong person reminds me of the importance of communication. That enabled me to learn that the number of people present during that 'teasing' or tempting conversation to attract the attention of a ghost must be kept to a minimum to avoid the ghost becoming confused about who to go with.

For me it's interesting to note the difference and the similarity between some of these examples. Consider for a moment the thought that if you are devoutly religious, a complete atheist or a murderer, you can get stuck and lost after death. It's quite ironic that these three types of people, so different in life, could get stuck in the same boat.

Interesting also is the concept of only seeing what we believe we can see and not what is there. By this I mean the farrier's situation, of being in the same haunted building, but unable to see even the other ghosts occupying the same space. There may be many different dimensions to the world of ghosts that make this possible.

So I expect the sinner, religious and atheist types of ghost may also be unable to see each other. An interesting idea.

In our consideration of our children and those with diminished comprehension perhaps it is our responsibility to educate them so that they can recognise when they have 'lost their bodies'. Then they would be able to move automatically to the spirit world, as I believe most dying people do. If we teach our children that death is a natural part of our Spiritual growth and something to celebrate and feel comfortable about, perhaps eventually we could end the cycle of ghosts and hauntings.

When you reflect on the incidents recorded of people who have survived a near death experience, often they have described their family and friends who have already died, standing by their beds, as if waiting for them. For most people I believe we are greeted by our relatives and guided straight over to the spirit world. Later in this book there is a section on the kind of situations that make it easier to become a ghost.

Fourteen

GHOST EXPECTATIONS

What happens if ghosts are not rescued?

If the ghosts are left to wander and find their own release from confusion, they can roam around for literally hundreds of years. Many a battle is still being fought, where the soldiers are so busy or shocked that they haven't noticed their own death. These battles can go on for many generations as evidenced by Peter's story and the ghost of the soldier from the London apartment (both referred to earlier in the book).

After a time, ghosts can bump into other ghosts and form sort of confused friendships, making the most of each other's company and the fun available. Sometimes they'll play tricks on us bodied people, because they can get to feel quite bitter about the way we seem to ignore them and they want to have as much enjoyment as they can.

If they are very strong individuals they may adopt a living body as their own. There is talk of ghosts getting trapped in our aura if they come too close. Coming too close could be caused by a ghost getting quite interested in our lives, like watching a television soap opera. They may hang around with us so much that they begin to occupy our space, to move into our bodies.

This is often referred to as 'spirit possession' and is feared by many as a demonic phenomena. I accept it as a sort of possession, which is a very good name for it, as the ghost sincerely believes that the body belongs to him, is his possession.

As far as a demonic phenomena is concerned, this is not the case. The poor ghost is so confused, that he simply thinks the body is his and can get quite upset if you suggest otherwise. When there is a conflict between the possessing ghost and the body's true owner, illness can result from the internal fight over the body.

Often possessing ghosts simply borrow the body, or win possession of it for short periods. This can cause the strange and somewhat unnerving experience of suddenly finding yourself somewhere strange and you don't remember how you got there.

An example would be sitting at home at 2pm then the next thing you know, you're in the town centre at 5pm without a coat or wearing slippers, and you don't know why or how you got there.

People are frequently considered mentally ill when this happens, unfortunately I don't believe our treatment of the mentally ill is able to effectively identify or deal with spirit possession. Perhaps this will change in the future – I certainly hope so.

Possession and mental health

Some people, it seems, are so confused after death that they wander around and even find themselves in the body of a (materially) living person. Spirit possession is often as innocent as that: a person just like you or me, a little confused after death, just wandering into someone else and taking them over because they've left their body and maybe believe this new one is really their own.

During one of the Wickland's seances in the 1920's, a possessing entity communicated through Mrs Wickland. The ghost wouldn't believe that he was dead or even borrowing someone else's body – he thought Mrs Wickland's body was his own.

He was encouraged to look at the hands and chest of the body to see he was in the form of a woman yet he was a man. After this, the spirit 'opened his mind' and accepted his situation and, looking for relatives, found them and went away to the 'other' world.

The wise Mr Wickland, drew the ghost's attention to the hands of the medium and to the breasts on the chest. The ghost found it hard to explain how he was inside the body of a woman and began to listen to reason. This opening of the ghost's mind eventually paved the way for him to accept that he had died and moved on to the Spirit World. The rescue of the ghost enabled a mental patient, who had been possessed by the entity, to recover to her normal condition.

To me it seems that many mental patients may simply be possessed, which is easy to cure and not only cures the patient but can also help the possessing spirit. This area merits further study to see if we can treat our patients better. So often our society seems to give up with the mentally ill, brushing the problem under the carpet. Exorcism of possessing ghosts, may prove an effective way of curing patients.

With alcohol too, it seems clear to me that people often get possessed. How often have you heard people say "He's a different person when he's been drinking"? How true is that? I've seen people who really do let someone else in when they are drinking. Would that explain why some people remember nothing about the evening after a certain period? Perhaps they were there but they were not in charge of their body at the time?

These lost souls are in a situation that resembles as closely as I can imagine 'purgatory' and is a situation of their own making. A self-imposed darkness that, with a little open-thinking and awareness, is avoidable.

Fortunately these people who get lost are in the minority, which is a great comfort to those who have been bereaved. I bet most of us get through, but I do care so much that we get away from any strong conceptions or, worst still, misconceptions about religion or afterlives. The more open our minds to the future beyond, then the faster we can accept our new state.

If you want to read a few more case studies get into 'The Unquiet Dead' by American psychologist Dr. Edith Fiore. She treats mental patients through hypnotism and exorcism thus addressing the patients other personalities or 'possessing' spirits and sending them away from her patients. It's good to see medical science catching on, she's now involved in training other psychiatrists to use her techniques and she acknowledges how well they work, whether or not you attach a religious belief to them or not.

Interesting, I hope you agree. I cannot recommend Dr Fiore's book highly enough but get this: I bought and read her book in Australia and gave it away to someone who needed it more than I did. I wanted a copy for my own reference but not until I'd got home from my round the world travels, you don't need too many books in a rucksack. So when I got home to England I ordered the book, or tried to, it was not available. Not listed. I even phoned the publisher in America asking how I can buy a copy in the UK "We don't supply that book in the UK". There's an address at the back of this book for a company who will obtain Dr Fiore's book to order.

Fifteen

DANGERS TO WATCH FOR

Alcohol, drugs and addictions

If you are addicted to cigarettes or drinking alcohol now that you are 'alive', it's my belief that you will still crave for these things when you're dead.

From the very first seance I went to I was given strict instructions not to drink before the session. When I enquired exactly why that was so important, I was simply told that if I turned up after alcohol I would attract drunk ghosts who can be particularly difficult to get through to. Just, I suppose, as it's difficult to get through to a drunk 'living' person, I can see that a 'dead drunk' would be hard to communicate with.

Although I didn't drink before a session, we'd often relax over a bottle of wine afterwards and have a general laugh and a chat.

In my reading though, I came across pretty detailed reports of drunks communicating at seances, often after possessing people and not really surprisingly having turned the possessed person to drink.

Some of this reading was care of Wickland, once again, and goes back to between 1894 and 1924 when his book was first published. It frustrated me, and still does to a degree, that this man made such detailed research and study which has hardly ever been widely available.

He found that some drunks died, and not knowing they'd died would hang around bars wanting a drink. Their desire for alcohol belonged to their souls not to the flesh that had died. They would possess someone who perhaps popped in for a quick drink after work and they would turn that into an all night drinking session, much to the surprise of the possessed person's friends.

Now I have friends who'll probably use that as an excuse when they are late home for dinner after a 'quick' drink in the pub, "Sorry dear, I must have got possessed by a very thirsty ghost". Some of my friends can find a laugh in almost anything.

But on the serious side, it is a bit alarming to think of those times when people, (and I've had them myself) simply have no recollection of what happened the night before. I am convinced that on those occasions they were being operated by someone else. Alcohol seems to lower our resistance to possession and make us very vulnerable. I am just grateful that once possessed we regain our sobriety, although I wonder if having found us susceptible to their influence whether the drunk ghost then tries to make us go back to the pub.

Very serious danger this possession business – it's much more common than most people realise and not as dramatic or noticeable as in the film 'The Exorcist' where heads revolve right round and all that demonic stuff.

I often hear the expression "he's a different person when he's had a drink" and I do not underestimate our powers of perception and I bet whoever says that knows exactly what is going on even if only on an unconscious level. If we pay attention to the choice of words a clear leak of knowledge from the astute and perceptive unconscious, to the conscious mind, can be observed. The truth of the observation is well worth contemplating.

I can think of loads of other examples where the choice of words used in communication is an indication of greater truth than is actually intended to be consciously expressed. An opportunity I offered a friend, involved him agreeing to do something that he didn't know much about, and his answer was "I am afraid I will have to decline your kind invitation". The man was telling me that unconsciously he was afraid, he didn't know what would be expected of him, and he likes to be in control.

Another area where language is telling more than we initially realise is 'organ speak'. An example of this being where someone is fed up and says "I can't stomach any more of it" and finds they get a stomach ulcer or indigestion. Someone else may say "I haven't got the heart for it" and develop heart trouble.

At a party in 1989, I met a young couple who didn't get on too well when the chap had been drinking. His girlfriend was actually a little scared of him when he'd been drinking, she said that his personality seemed to change. He even seemed different to me, and I was drinking too.

She was an example of someone saying "He's a different person after a drink". I asked her for more details and we got chatting about my view that he may become possessed after alcohol. This theory seemed to fit her perception of how he was and she asked what could be done. I had been drinking too so I couldn't attempt a rescue that evening. I did suggest that if he became a little violent or behaved out of character that it would not be unreasonable for her to tell whoever was possessing her boyfriend to "go away and leave them both alone."

It seemed a bit of a long shot to me but was the best I could think of in the middle of a party.

The next morning was a truly beautiful day, getting out of my tent was a sheer joy... blue sky and, a real bonus, a clear head. The young girl came to talk to me over breakfast and described the amazing events once she was alone with her boyfriend the previous night.

Yes, he got a bit aggressive and strange so she'd asked, as I'd suggested, whoever was in her boyfriend to "Go away, leave my boyfriend alone". Then a bigger surprise, her boyfriend started talking in different voices and she had to tell five clearly different personalities or spirit entities to go away.

You could've knocked me down with a feather or heard my jaw hit the floor. I was amazed that things had gone so well. Besides that, when the five possessing spirits finally went, her boyfriend was back to normal and seemed to know what had happened. They spoke about his drinking and his apparent 'possession behaviour' for the first time. He confided that his father had always had a drink problem and he wondered if the spirits had always been around.

Anyway, I was so pleased that they had been able to resolve their difficulties that I gave them my copy of 'The Unquiet Dead', which includes an extremely good section on alcohol and drug abuse. I thought it would also be an inspiration to them to continue their discussion and help to keep the chap off the alcohol.

Wickland also devoted part of his book ('Thirty Years Among the Dead') to the danger of drug and alcohol addiction and I would like to quote an example from that section.

To quote the spirit of Wallace R., who said the following during a conversation through the psychic Mrs Wickland, on October 17th 1923 about drug abuse having died as an addict:

"I wish I could warn many I knew and tell them not to play with drugs. They think it is fun in the beginning, but how they will have to suffer to the last! Even the soul burns from the craving. They should do everything they can to overcome the habit.

"They not only suffer here, (meaning material plane) but they suffer terribly after they pass out; then the soul is on fire.

"Many, yes, many, come back and try to ruin others against their will. I knew many times that I myself did not want it, but there was such a strong power back of me. If the world could only know!"

Powerful stuff from someone who recognised that even when he was an addict he was possessed, sometimes when he had that strong power "back of me". He wanted his message heard loud and clear so I quote him here. He comments further on alcohol, which I also mention because some drug users justify what they do by referring to how their parents drink. Wallace R. had been in the movie industry and after death he recognised the damage done by Prohibition in the USA and he goes on to say:

"When people drink it makes them drunk, but after a good sleep they get over it, and they do not have the terrible craving that they do from drugs.

"The world will go mad if the narcotic evil is not stopped soon. Shutting out liquor did great harm, because people must have a stimulant of some kind. They work hard, very hard, in the movies, and it is nerve racking work. As I said, they must have something to stimulate their nerves so they can go on.

"If they took some wine, or beer, or even some whiskey, to quiet their nerves, it would not be such a detriment as morphine."

Another book, which I refer to and really value, is 'The Nature of Personal Reality' by Jane Roberts and the reason I mention it here is this: the book was dictated entirely by Seth, a spirit, through Jane Roberts, a medium. Nothing so unusual about that except that Jane Roberts drinks beer for relaxation whilst she is in trance. So alcohol in moderation cannot be all bad but I think it is important to be aware of the dangers. Not just to our bodies, which I believe can be amazingly adaptable, but also to our own spiritual consciousness. If we take too many drugs then I believe we may dull our own psychic awareness and weaken the power of our intuition as well as becoming vulnerable to spirit possession.

When Carl Wickland was working back in the early twentieth century, he found some possessing entities so hard to communicate with that he used to administer small electric shocks to the medium, his wife, to get their full attention.

Now I have no experience of rescuing drunk spirits personally so I can only recommend further reading on this subject. It does, however, seem well worth avoiding a situation where you can be possessed by such a determined or confused ghost that it takes an electric shock to get their attention. One way to avoid such a situation is to avoid excess drink and drugs.

The rescues I've dealt with were really straightforward because the ghosts listened, grasped the point that they were dead and saw the advantages of going on to a new dimension. The ones I read about in Wickland's book were still craving for a drink and often interrupted the rescue pleading for a glass of bourbon whiskey, "just a small one". Well I can see how difficult it would be to get through to a ghost like that.

In addition to the danger of getting possessed when you drink excessively, or take drugs, what happens if you die in that state? What if you stagger across the road very drunk and get knocked down by a car? Will you wander off, away from your body for another drink in the nearest bar? How long can the cycle go on? How many generations could be afflicted through excess alcohol and drug abuse?

Some of my pals will laugh their heads off when they read this because they've seen me have more than one drink and will think this is a bit hypocritical. Yes, I guess it is. At least I know a little about the risks. Also I believe I would recognise a possessing ghost and could perform the rescue process myself, as I did when I had the headache inflicted on me in the earlier example. It is important to know your limits when it comes to alcohol.

I am very concerned for the people who know that alcohol or drugs are damaging their health and still consume them. They seem to have the attitude "I'd rather carry on drinking and die happy, than give up now and live a miserable life".

If only they could realise how miserable their After-Life could be if they do not master their addiction in their mortal life!

An addiction after death can cause so much sadness and confusion, not just for the dead addict but, as you've seen here, for those possessed people who fall victim to the cravings of the ghost and become dependent on drink or drugs.

Crime and drugs

Looking at Wickland again, there is a brilliant section written at a seance on July 26th 1922, which is Minnie Morgan's account of her recovery from morphine addiction and her reflections, as a spirit, on life twenty-five years after she died (as an addict).

In her account, she described how her need for the drug remained so strong after her body had died and goes into some horrific detail how she was so aware of wanting to be able to get drugs, that she remained so close to her body that she was aware of being 'dissected' (her post-mortem examination).

The awareness Minnie shares of her experience after recovering from the addiction and her perceptions of the spirit world and her values, is really fascinating. She also makes some sagacious comments on possession.

Whilst talking about crime and murder committed by a person who is possessed, Minnie Morgan said:

"A cunning spirit gets into this man's magnetic aura and controls him. He commits some crime. The man will hang for his deed, but he never did it. He will probably say: 'I must have been drunk when I did it, for I don't remember anything about it'."

"But it was not the liquor that did it. Liquor never does that. When a man is drunk his mind is in a stupor. It is a spirit that does the work."

Further comment by the same spirit:

"The majority of murders and hold-ups are committed by spirits. They scheme and scheme, and use mortals as tools, until they wake up and realise what wrong they have been doing."

Shocking stuff and the original two volumes of similar comment, documented accurately by Carl Wickland, is now available in one book and is listed in the Bibliography. There's loads of information available but it is hidden in specialist bookshops and libraries, so you really have to work hard to get hold of it. Once you enter a 'New Age' book shop there is so much choice it is hard to know where to begin. I hope the Bibliography and recommended reading list will be of assistance to you.

So once again, from these comments, we can see that the potential of possession can be awesome indeed. These possessing spirits are not evil though. They simply are carrying on as they were in their mortal lives. If they were bank robbers, drug addicts or drunks in their lives, then they will simply retain the same habits and desires when they die, especially if they don't know that they are dead.

This is one of the reasons that I believe it is so important that I write this book, so you will be aware of your state changing through strange experiences when you die. Then, whatever your life has been like, through knowledge that you are no longer mortally alive you will not seek to possess others or remain in the material plane.

You will have the choice available to progress into the spiritual dimension and learn more about your life and the new reality of your spirituality.

Grief and the danger of dabbling with spirit communication

If this book has inspired your curiosity and you now wish to go to seances then I suggest you hesitate and examine your beliefs and motivation before you begin.

In my work at rescue circles or seances, whilst I have enjoyed the pleasure of knowing that someone is rescued often after many years of their having been confused, I have been doing it largely for the benefit of those spirits unable to find their own way without such help.

Also, I had been going with commitment – I think I went every Monday evening for around three or four years. A big commitment for an adolescent who enjoyed his social life and had college work or girlfriends to look after. Even now, I am told off by the spirit guides if I am late sitting or miss the regular time. I imagine they go to a great deal of trouble preparing to bring lost ghosts to the circle for rescuing and must be quite vexed if we are not around as expected.

I would not recommend going to a seance to find answers either – the answer is nearly always inside you and that's the best place to look. The knowledge that can be obtained from spirit communication has been clearly documented in many 'channelled' books and is available without going to a seance. If you want personally tailored answers or input on questions about your life or problems, I suggest you use a pendulum; there is a section on how to use one later in the book and I believe this may be helpful.

To go to a seance to be reunited with lost relatives is a common reason for going and that's up to you. For myself I hardly ever expect to talk to anyone I knew. They have their own lives to lead. We've agreed that they are gone; let them go without hassle. It must be tough to die and see the people you love grieving so much. I know when I die I'll be pleased to know that my family and friends cared about me but I don't want to see them spoil their day over it. Each of us has our own life and why upset someone else's if you can avoid it.

A lot of that grief is over unexpressed truth or love. You know the sort of thing "I never did tell him how much I loved him". So why not make a commitment to express more love and truth to everyone to avoid grieving as much as possible. It may even make life more rewarding too, who knows?

After death, I would not want to be pulled back to see a sad familiar face at a seance, someone I loved, who I would see cannot manage too well without me. I'd be really sad, disappointed and worried that I had left them in the lurch. I'd much rather think that my loved ones would respect my choice to die and let me get on with it and learn to live happily without me.

There is a philosophy I hold, which goes like this:

If we grieve the passing of a loved one too much it hinders their ability to leave the material plane. Because we want them back, so they find it hard to go.

In the Arthur Conan Doyle book, mentioned earlier, he is quoted as saying "There is work to be accomplished in the next world which cannot be done if the spirit is continually being held back by those who mourn its passing" and "The fault arises when there is clinging by earthly people to an arisen soul which should pass onward". I recommend reading the book "The Return of Arthur Conan Doyle" if you wish to see the full context of these two quotes. The message is clear, we should let our loved ones go with our blessing and love.

You can bet your life that when I go, boy am I going! I don't intend to hang around, I want to go on ahead and find out more of what's going on. I'll catch up with a few friends who went on ahead of me and set up a few parties for my mates who will, one day, follow on. Then I'll want to get to work, explore and learn about the 'other side'.

I am also curious to discover how I'll really feel about what I have done with this life. How will I judge myself when I am back in the Spirit World? I am also curious about what I already knew from my past lives that I forgot when I was born this time. It'll be interesting to be myself again, but I am in no tearing rush as there is still a lot that I wish to achieve before I die.

Anyway, the sort of stuff I reckon people get at seances from relatives is a bit odd. I mean what do you talk about to someone you loved who has died? Can you imagine "Have you seen your Gran? How's the budgie that died, is he up there? Has he got new feathers? Does he still like his bell?"

Would my Dad be interested in what I've been doing? And if he was he can have a look, can't he? He doesn't need to be dragged to a seance to know what I'm doing. If he can influence my evenings by becoming visible to people, as you'll read in a later example, then he's got access to more than enough knowledge already without me telling him anything.

Also, what can our dead relatives say to us? We wouldn't understand what their world is like. If you were really interested in trying to understand what the Spirit World is like, then you'd have sought out and read some of the many channelled books which attempt to describe it.

It's better, I believe, to let loved ones go with our blessing. The best thing we can do, is to wish them well and tidy up any of their loose ends that they may worry about. The more quickly we get happy again the faster and better they can build their new lives.

Don't get me wrong, I love my Dad and I am sure he knows that, just as if you lose someone, they'll know how you feel. You don't have to go to a seance for that.

If you set up a seance yourself with a ouija board, or bits of card arranged alphabetically and an upturned glass, as I did at school, then watch out. Or better still don't do it and if you must at least don't take the results too seriously.

Try to remember the importance of all the people present saying

The Lord's Prayer and that a specific prayer for protection and guidance must also be said. I'll include an example of a protection prayer later.

The purpose of these prayers seems to be to focus the conscious and unconscious minds of those present to attract only benevolent spirits and not pranksters or drunks. Drunk and addicted ghosts are, from my study of Wickland's work, very hard to deal with. Not because they are evil or wish any harm. They don't seem ready to listen and they are likely to say anything to attempt to satisfy the craving that still exists after their death. In the time I have been attending seances I have found that these prayers do work and I see no reason to experiment with another method.

Having had a particularly shocking event take place through this sort of game when I was about thirteen I can only warn you not to do it or to ignore the consequences.

Firstly, I believe that the more simple the method of communication the easier it is for any old spirit to come for a chat at your seance. Secondly, there is no simpler way to communicate than for a spirit to move a glass when it's got three or four children's fingers on it. Piece of cake for most of them. This means that any spirit or even ghost can come along and either add his finger, if he's a ghost and thinks he's still got fingers of his own, or influence someone else's if he's a spirit.

Now, who would come along to such a simple gathering of playful inquisitive children?

Yes, you've got it. A playful, inquisitive ghost or spirit. Just as we may have a sense of fun or even mischief, we don't necessarily lose that when we die. Our personality is as strong as ever.

So what sort of fun and games does our ghostly visitor have with us? What would amuse him? Would he enjoy startling us? Making us gasp with shock? Making us giggle nervously, maybe even frighten us?

Yes of course, that's just what the kids want isn't it? They want something shocking that they can keep secret and wouldn't dare tell their parents. "They'd never believe us would they?"

I can remember it and picture it so clearly. I wonder how many adults today didn't play those games and cannot understand this very clearly.

We got well into it and some of my friends did it fanatically. We even spoke to Hitler or someone who said he was Hitler and scared the pants off us. How ridiculous that Hitler would have time to drop by to a kids' seance in Hertfordshire. He's probably got enough on his plate trying to get all those people he wronged to forgive him.

It's so easy for a spirit to say he's Hitler and boy, does that get a reaction from the kids? It's about as simple as a Punch and Judy show and not half as valuable.

Once, when I was aged thirteen, I was not at the house where we did the ouija board stuff, they carried on regardless and gave themselves a fright.

Apparently they got this ghost through and started asking about things that would happen in the future. Dramatic stuff, especially when they were told I was going to die in six months.

Well they were all freaked out. "What do we do now?" and all that drama. They agreed to keep it a secret, no one must tell Lance.

But, kids are kids and someone did tell me. So I freaked out for a day or two and then ignored it. A load of rubbish, I decided. Fortunately I had already learnt by then of the frivolous nature of some ghosts who are able to enter an 'unprotected' seance and took the whole thing as a joke.

I didn't even think to exploit the dramatic value of having only six months to live. Probably just as well because I really do feel that if you believe that sort of prediction you can bring about your own death. I believe that we do each create our own realities. If you believe hard enough that you're going to die in six months then there isn't a lot that can stop you dying.

What you believe you get: especially with matters of health and death. I always wondered why some fit men died on squash courts at thirty to forty-five years old. It seemed too young to die of exercise. Now I wonder if those adults ever said what I heard children say when I was at school "I don't want to die of old age" – "I don't want to be old" or some similar statement. If so, their beliefs may have created what they got, an early death. It is so important to guide our beliefs to get what we want.

So be careful kids, playing with ghosts can be a whole bag of worms if you mess it up and believe it. At the end of the day you're going to get better value out of confiding in someone who is alive, in mortal terms, if you want to talk about an area of confusion in your life. If you just want a laugh, why not play a joke on a friend who's alive and who'll appreciate it? Then you can share the joke with everyone and not keep it a secret. Or you could go to Punch and Judy.

If you want advice from another source, you'd be well advised to get a pendulum and use your own dowsing skills to give you an additional perspective. There is a section on how to do this later in the book, but the pendulum will swing one way for yes and another for no, thereby giving answers from either your unconscious or from the spirit guides, depending on your belief.

If you want to know about what's going to happen in the future write down exactly what you want to happen in the future and go for that. Do all you can to get the future to fit in with you. So few people do that, you'll probably get your own way. More about this though in the books on Visualisation, see the Bibliography and I may have written one by the time you read this.

If you want a long healthy life, picture what you'd like to be doing when you are eighty years old and how fit and prosperous you will be. How much fun will you be having? Create a vision of your future so you can erase any passing negative belief you held long ago.

Anyway, that was over twenty years ago and I'm still going strong.

Lance's fake ghost picture

How to protect yourself from ghosts

As far as I can tell, you're as safe as you want to be. If you believe that you are safe, then you are. If you want to feel in danger then feel you are and you will be.

The ghosts that are attracted to you will directly reflect your own feelings. Just as earlier I proposed that if a playful group of frivolous, adolescent, children play with a ouija board they'll get only playful frivolous spirits coming to communicate with them.

If you feel the hairs on the back of your neck stand up or feel the room go slightly colder and maybe even sense that there is some other presence in your room, just assume that you're safe, no harm is meant. You will be safe, remember that most ghosts are just confused people. You could even acknowledge the ghost with the words "God Bless You. Do you know that you're a ghost? I know you're there but cannot see or hear you. You'd be better off thinking of a friend or relative who's dead too, so that you can see them and go to the spirit world. Have a look around, I bet you can see them."

Before you know it you'll be free of any fear and able to remain calm and feel strongly protected.

I was reflecting on this and realised that I felt more able to be relaxed when other people see ghosts simply because I didn't see or hear them, I just sense them. This gives me a sort of detachment and inner calm. I wondered if I might think that the ghost was really a person with a body if I saw them in addition to my present awareness of them.

A danger I do respect is more from a possessed person under the influence of drink or drugs, as discussed earlier, who has the physical ability to do harmful things, as it is harder to get the possessing entity to listen to reason.

So for protection and safety just feel safe, recognise that no ghost can harm you. If you use prayer to inspire that feeling of safety then do pray, and know that it works. You will be as safe as you feel.

To avoid possession the main thing is to be moderate with alcohol and avoid drugs like the plague. Once you become 'unconscious' you may be opening the door to possessing spirits. Believe that you are safe and free of possessing spirits and you will most likely be rid of them. The times when you do not remember anything, or have huge blank spots, from the night before you have possibly been possessed. If so, you can sit down quietly and give the possessing spirit a talking to, as I did after visiting Holland Park, and make it clear that they are in your body because they are dead. Then you can do the simple rescue procedure to help them on their way.

Here's another example of possession:

A quite psychic young man who was worried about his girlfriend was telling me how she would go home after work, go to her room intending to read. The next thing she knew she would 'wake up' in the High Street with no coat feeling cold having no recollection of how she got there or why she was there.

His concern, which at a later seance we found was justified, was that during her blackouts she was being possessed. He was worried that she may come to some harm, which I didn't feel was all that likely but was concerned for her and for the possessing spirit that was really wasting its own time interfering with her.

We did the rescue. Somehow she'd picked up a German U-Boat crew and they were delighted to be rescued having been in their submarine where they'd died during the second world war.

Her blackouts though are not that dissimilar to those of a heavy drinker who laughs about not recalling what happened the previous evening. "Did I really do that?" even surprised at some of the 'out of character' things he may have done. But still the penny doesn't drop and even now people will read this and say, "Nonsense, alcohol just makes you forget things. I'm not possessed I just enjoy a drink."

When you are under anaesthetic your mind is drugged and you are just as unconscious as when you, after a booze-up, cannot remember what happened. However someone else has been operating your body when you are unconscious from drinking if people tell you you've been doing things that you cannot remember.

Anyway, for your own curiosity why not read Wickland's book where the drunk spirits describe how they used to possess people and lead them into the bar for a good drink. That was back in the early 1900's but it is still going on today, probably even more widespread. Don't misunderstand, I like a drink myself but understand the risks involved and know how to clear myself of possessing entities should I attract any.

Dr Edith Fiore, in her book ('The Unquiet Dead'), describes a process that she calls 'The White Light Technique', for protecting yourself from possession. This technique involves imagining that you are a powerful source of protecting white light which emanates from your solar plexus and surrounds you with a protecting white aura. This method sounds excellent and should be used if it seems more natural to you than prayer.

Remember that you are safe, ghosts are just confused people in need of help. Would you hang around people that ignored you feeling lonely, rejected and unloved if you had the choice?

I suggest that another strong means of protection is to feel sympathy with the confused dead person and chat to them and help them understand their position and send them on their way.

Reincarnation is a belief that can cause possession

Some people believe that when they die, they will instantly be reborn as a young child or baby.

I don't agree with them and I suggest that there is merit in dropping that belief, even if it is partly true.

When we die, I believe that before we are reincarnated, if we are at all, we return to the Spirit World to discuss how we got on down here. We have a sort of counselling session with other Spirits who can advise us on where we may feel we could have done better. A sort of Spiritual debriefing.

Once that's complete and we've recovered from the effects of having a body, I believe we get the chance to decide whether or not we wish to come back here to complete and unfinished lessons.

Then, the process of being reincarnated begins, once a path is located that will give us the tests and lessons that we need to learn from. A process that probably does not happen overnight. I expect it could be quite complicated deciding who is to be born where and to whom, the sort of parents, the sex of the child etc.

The difficulty that can be caused by the belief that the reincarnation process is instant is this:

Some people die, realise that they are dead, don't look around them to notice the wonderful light of love waiting to guide them to the Spirit World. The reason these people don't notice the Pearly light, is that they are looking for a way to get into a new body. They believe that they must seek out a baby to live and have another life.

So, these people are harmless but can cause themselves to possess a baby, simply that is what they believe must happen!

So, I suggest you drop that picture if you have it and open to other possibilities!

Sixteen

WHY DO WE HAVE GHOSTS?

From the examples of the different rescues, you can see that ghosts occur for a variety of reasons, ranging from a rigid expectation of the events that 'should' take place after death, to a fixed opinion that there is no after life.

There is also the person who has lead a bad life and feels so guilty, that even if he knows he's dead will still hide and avoid going to any other form of spirit life. This example contradicts the original definition of ghosts and spirits, perhaps as this person knows he's dead this is what we should identify as an earthbound spirit. He is earthbound by his belief about the nature of the after-life, but it is his own choice to be so bound. He is not fixed here as a punishment by anyone else, he is doing it to himself.

The drug and alcohol abusers can be in such a disoriented state that they wouldn't recognise their own death and they must be very confused when they die. From earlier examples, it was apparent that they can still crave for their addiction, that can enable them to get stuck in a confused state. A drunk can die and remain in a bar with living drunk people, where his influence can make the situation worse for everyone, dead and living, as he encourages increased alcohol intake.

How hard it must be to give up a drinking habit if every time you have just one drink, a possessing spirit turns up craving alcohol and tips more drinks down you.

Another potential cause of earthbound spirits is the over zealous grief and mourning of the death of a loved one. I really wish our belief in the after life was strong enough for us to celebrate the death of a friend. After all, they don't have to worry about the recession or see bad news on television. They are with old friends and in a world of love, so why should we be so miserable? Of course we miss them but we could at least wish them a happy time.

The danger is, that we appear so helpless and lost when we grieve, that they may want to stay to help us. In focusing their attention on our material world, they may loose the ability or opportunity to see the spirit world and so become earthbound. Imagine all the old relatives and chums coming to greet our dear departed and he just looks at the mourners, wishing he could tell them that he's survived death. That must be very frustrating for the spirits who have come to guide the departed person over to the spirit world.

War can create ghosts. As soldiers fight and exist in fear of dying, they are so busy trying to survive, that they can go on thinking they are alive even after they are killed. They continue fighting the war long after they've died. Even after the war is over soldiers will be fighting their battles as ghosts. The example of the soldiers earlier in the book highlight this event. The price of war is much higher than the death and suffering we see. The price can still be being paid by the dead soldiers centuries later.

What do all these different causes of ghosts have in common?

The sinner, religious maniac, addicts and the children all have the same lack of awareness. No teaching has been given on the value of being open to the possibility of death being like sleep and what to expect when we wake up after death.

The sinner, the religious fanatic and the atheist all have a fixed idea about the world beyond and that fixed image prevents them seeing what is really there. Their ignorance of the possibilities keeps them lost in the purgatory of the world between worlds. Whether they know that they are dead or not, makes no real difference to the value of their existence if they are stuck in that nomansland in between lives.

So the cause of getting lost seems to be ignorance, lack of openness to new and unexpected possibilities. Surely in this life an openness to new possibilities is a valuable asset, which helps us get most out of this life. So why not encourage that enthusiasm for the unexpected to be applied to death and the hereafter? Surely we cannot know exactly what it's like to die or exactly who will be there to greet us. So why teach rigid views based on metaphorical teaching and belief?

From my research I have formed many opinions about the after-life and what it may be like in the spirit world. But I know that we cannot really understand what that world is like, because we think in the context of our earthly life. Anyway, what does it matter to us now, what the qualities of the spirit world may be?

The important thing is for us to live as though we will be moving to some other life and keep an open mind, remembering how to recognise when we die and know at least one way to find our way to the spirit world if we get lost.

Seventeen

MORE ON SPIRIT COMMUNICATION

Since I first began to sit at seances regularly there have been many large catastrophes involving vast loss of life. Here I recall earthquakes, floods, famine, hurricanes, typhoons, war and the Zeebrugge ferry capsize.

Now one thing I've always found a little tricky to comprehend, which I have come across when I sit and in nearly all my reading and study, is the idea that time is a concept that belongs to us and is created by us. The idea further proposes that spirits do not have time, all things happen simultaneously.

This idea stretches my brain in about three dimensions at once and still I find it hard to comprehend. Apparently also, all our incarnations are occurring simultaneously. At the same time you may be living in the twentieth century you could also be living as a Pharaoh in ancient Egypt, a beggar in the Industrial Revolution and a peasant farmer. Well I don't know about you but I'm not ready to try to get my head round all that. If you want to study this further then read your way through the Bibliography, and if you get to fit it in your head drop me a line or write a book about it, I'd be fascinated.

The reason for mentioning time is that when there is to be a disaster, the spirit people already know of its implications and prepare themselves for it.

There would be occasions when we'd get ourselves settled on a Monday night for the regular circle and we'd open with prayer as usual, greet the usual guides and then get a clear message.

"We will be brief tonight, we are preparing for further work". We'd get the message and close the circle early.

Next day there would be a typhoon in Asia or something similar. Sometimes we'd sit and the disaster may have taken place and our spirit guides would say "We must close early as we are going to help".

Our own guides would be going off to help rescue the dying, to help them 'over' to the next dimension as they leave their bodies. It's quite incredible, I know, but that's what was happening at our circle.

With the Zeebrugge Ferry disaster in 1987, the spirit people worked so hard and so well that they actually got every single spirit 'over'. There were no lost souls or ghosts trapped in the ferry. I mention this phenomenon as I trust it will help the bereaved to know that their relatives are helped when they die. All this talk in earlier sections of how easy it can be to become a ghost, well there is a lot of effort that goes into preventing it too.

The vast scale of the 'spirit aid' that goes into a disaster is quite incredible. If spirits communicating in Hertfordshire, England are rushing as volunteers to all parts of the world from Asia to Ethiopia and Chernobyl to Zeebrugge then I assume spirits from all over are also helping.

The other point on time. As spirits just think they are somewhere, and then they are there, they are not limited by night or day so they have little need for time. Their lack of time becomes quite clear when they are giving guidance concerning what we call 'future' events. The spirit people talk in terms of soon, shortly, in a while, in the next few seasons. They find it difficult to pin point, in our terms of time, exactly when an event will occur.

In view of the time thing, I am concerned that psychics should not be taken too literally or criticised if what they say will happen, does not happen exactly when they say it will. Their source of information is having the same difficulty, time is our province and not the spirits'.

Also I presume we can, following a psychic prediction, influence the rate of manifestation of any particular factor described by the psychic, thus making any time prediction inaccurate, even if it was correct in the first place.

Anyway, enough regarding time, this section was about the vast amount of spiritual assistance given all the time and particularly when world disasters occur. I found this discovery particularly reassuring as I have always believed that help is as important for the dead as it is for the survivors.

It eases the tragedy, for at least we know that the people who die are going on to begin a new adventure.

Disaster as a demonstration to others

Even war serves as motivation towards peace and is therefore of some value to us, who survive it. Without the wars in our world we would perhaps forget what a terrible ordeal we put our families through when our Nations refuse to compromise.

If it wasn't for the dreadful Vietnam war, the Gulf war could have been the same long, drawn-out battle with many more deaths and even greater suffering. Having said this, I do appreciate that technological advances in warfare, the lack of forest ground cover and increased satellite intelligence all played a significant part in the decisive results of the conflict in Kuwait.

This does not of course mean imagining disasters are good, but if they are going to happen, I believe it's healthy to find some value from them. At least learn something constructive, like preventing a ferry sailing with its door open.

There was a young boy killed in a motor accident near my home town and the value created from that tragedy has been the motivation of an action group who have succeeded in getting the black-spot junction changed. This could save the lives of many children and adults in years to come.

Through the suffering of the 'smoking beagles', brought to the attention of the public in 1975, we are now more concerned about animal welfare and a market has evolved for products that have not been tested on animals. If the beagles had not suffered severe cruelty for the frivolous whim of smoking, perhaps we would have felt less motivated to protest and milder forms of experiment would have gone unchecked.

The loss of trees in October 1989 prompted greater attention to our environment through planting and conservation. Let's face it, those trees would have fallen over on their own eventually but the value of losing them all at once was probably worthwhile for the lessons it taught us.

The loss of my father when I was a young boy, seemed a vast price but later I could see the value in terms of increased compassion and awareness of the losses of others. His death served as the final straw in a history of fatal accidents and led to a new road layout, thus giving value to others.

Manifestations and phenomena

During the time I have been writing this book, I have been progressing with the rescue work to assist lost Ghosts and Spirits. This has meant that there have been times when a ghost may turn up at my home and hang around until the next time I sit with the purpose of helping Ghosts to move on.

These Ghosts are not always silent visitors, sometimes they make their presence known.

Some time ago I was watching a program on television about an old soldier returning to the area where he fought during the First World War. He went on this visit, I think annually, to meet up with the French families who had helped him during those difficult years.

The program was a but sombre and I confess I was losing interest in watching it. As you may expect, I picked up the remote control and turned the television off and then strolled from the lounge through the hall and into the kitchen. I wanted to see how long there was before dinner, so I could see what best to do with the time available.

Dinner was imminent so I decided to just sit and read in the lounge and off I went, back to the lounge.

Imagine my surprise to find that the television was on! The same program about the First World War was still running.

"Okay" I said to myself, perhaps I'm meant to watch this program. I was the only person in the house apart from my fiancee, who was in the kitchen. Nobody could have turned the television on.

Eventually the program ended and I turned the television off with the remote control and went to the dining room for dinner.

The incidents of the television coming on by itself continued. My fiancee was as confident as I was that Spirits or Ghosts were causing the phenomenon. When we next sat the Spirit People confirmed that the television was being sort of 'bumped into' by the energy of passing ghosts.

We were not worried by this and simply found it slightly amusing. The television would come on when we were not in the lounge, sometimes it seemed as though a ghost had wanted to watch the cartoons.

The television would also turn on when we were in the lounge and we became quite used to the event. Some of our friends, however, were quite startled by this and found are ambivalence just as shocking.

"It's ok" we'd say "it's just someone passing through".

One friend suggested, quite reasonably, that it may be a fault on the television. I was able to tell him of a time when the television came on, quite loudly, when I was busy concentrating in the dining room. The dining room and lounge doors were both open and I was startled by the loud noise.

"Turn that off at once." I said sternly, in the direction of the lounge. The television did turn off, immediately. There was no one in the lounge so nobody could have operated the control.

That was when I gave up any possibility that I had a faulty television. The television still comes on *by itself* – months can go by without a single thing happening, then the television will be off and on quite often. I noticed the other day, that whilst the television will turn itself on and off on its own while I'm in the lounge, it will never turn off by itself, if I've turned it on. Mind you, it might come on when the house is empty and go off again as I arrive home.

Another thing that happened, which I didn't take such a relaxed approach to was with the garage door. This has is electrically operated and has a remote control that allows me to open or close the door from my car. Well, during the peak of the television activity, I was in the dining room with my fiancée when we heard a strange noise. It was like a motor running some gear wheels. It took me a while to realise that what I could hear was the sound of the garage door opening!

I quickly went to the garage and yes, the door was opening.

"Look here! That just is not appropriate or acceptable" I stated firmly to the Spirit presence that I assumed was responsible for opening the door.

"If that happens when I am out, I could be inviting someone to steal bicycles and tools. That must not happen again!"

Fortunately, the garage door never has opened or closed on its own again. This too makes me feel less inclined to believe in the normal explanations, as if it was faulty, surely the door and television would still operate on their own?

The Spirit People did confirm that the garage door had been operated in the same way as had the television.

Spiritual inspiration and intervention

If you believe any of this stuff about spirits rescue circles and seances, part of you must want to ask things about you and your life. You must have things you'd like help with and to know more about, perhaps even know the outcome of certain things.

Well here's my advice, don't bother too much about knowing. These spirit people are pretty adept at influencing events if they wish and frankly so are we. Use a pendulum in the way described later to get answers to your questions from deep within yourself.

The most important thing I could say about the future is that you create it yourself (there's a mass on this subject in the Seth books, see the Bibliography) and whatever predictions are made don't matter unless you are willing to play your part in creating the outcome, by believing that the result you want will occur.

That may mean that if you believe in poverty you'll be poor or in sickness you'll be ill. So the main thing is to deal with your own beliefs, examine them and if you want to change your life, do it through changing your beliefs.

The help that I've had in my life from spirits is probably quite vast but I feel most of it comes through my own intuition as it does to anyone, whether or not they believe in this stuff or not.

In situations where I really have been unsure and the spirits have invited me to ask questions about my life, which I never do unless invited to, the answer has always been "Listen to your intuition, do what you believe is right, your intuition is always correct".

Powerful stuff and I suggest you try it, just do what you first think of from your intuition, don't rationalise to the point where you talk yourself out of an action that was inspired by your intuition. Ignore that inner voice of your mind that says such things as "What if it doesn't work?" "You might just make yourself look stupid?" "But they might not want to speak to you". Ignore all that rubbish. Your mind is such a weed when it tries to stop you taking action and risks.

From a book on NLP (Neuro-Linguistic Programming see bibliography), I learnt a little about one of the mind's greatest responsibilities. Its main job is to keep us safe. You can imagine what a big responsibility and challenge that is for the mind. Now your mind has probably got parts that are as lazy as mine and in a perfect world the mind would like you to do today exactly what you did yesterday.

The mind knows for certain that you survived yesterday and that if you repeat yesterday every day, then you'll be safe and your mind can take it easy.

To encourage you to repeat safe, practiced patterns of behaviour, your mind gives you those inner voices, the ones that limit you and stop you taking risks. It's just your mind's way of looking after you. Your mind, the part that deals with safety, does not consider fun, boredom, expansion, growth or adventure.

Learn to ignore those voices that conflict with your intuition. At first you could ignore it once per day to practise. You know, the times when you want to say something spontaneously and don't because of your rational head. Well thank your head and tell it to support you in taking a risk.

Try taking a different route home each day or doing any routine in a new way. Eat at different times and taste new foods.

If you still get loads of limiting voices, tell your mind that it must get used to working harder, not limiting you but concentrating harder to make you quicker witted and more astute to adapt to the risks and intuition you choose to follow.

Of course, if your mind is helping you avoid life-threatening situations by saying "don't jump" or checking for traffic before crossing the road, don't ignore it! Use your common sense.

Anyway there is plenty of information about that available in 'Frogs Into Princes' and other books on NLP. See the Bibliography to find these books, NLP is fascinating.

Intuition helps

The following is an example of help through intuition, which surprised me.

Some years ago when I had a tough interview coming up with an employer I sat at a circle as usual and was invited to ask questions. I asked about the forthcoming meeting with my boss, and the spirit people simply said "Arrive in plenty of time for the meeting, turn off your car radio and just sit quietly in your car for five minutes before you go in and just relax."

Well I did what they said, I arrived early at the corporate headquarters and sat quietly in my car to tune in to my intuition.

The meeting was incredible. I was saying things that I didn't even know I knew about. But only after I said them, did I realise the strangeness of my knowledge. It's hard to describe exactly what I mean. Imagine a young enthusiastic salesman who really only cares about the thrill of making a sale, then imagine that salesman talking in terms of cash flow and profitability and presenting a strong case that he is able to produce sales and maximise profits.

Not too strange, you may think, but if you knew that young salesman it was unreal to imagine him in his naivety talking in such terms. After the meeting, which got me the result I was after, it dawned on me what had occurred and I was grateful to myself for my intuition although I do also acknowledge those spirits that may have inspired me.

That's exactly the sort of powerful experience that will result from trusting your own intuition, inspiration or sense of knowing.

I'm sure many of us can think of examples of similar guidance and can reflect on the source of that inspiration.

Another example of assistance where really I had to play the part myself was before writing this book.

Bearing in mind that many of my experiences related in this book concern other people and spirit guides, I thought I must check with the spirit people that they are ok about me writing it. I do believe that I was probably inspired by them to write it in the first place however.

I took myself to the coast to my old friends with whom I used to sit every week and asked to have a seance with them. Now, in my business work I was at the time concluding the biggest deal of my life and was pretty amazed at how fortunate I was being and how well the negotiations were going. This is relevant as you'll see in a moment.

The seance was in progress, after the usual prayers for protection, and there came a time when my questions were invited. Firstly I asked about the book, "Is it ok for me to write the book I want about rescue work and ghosts?" I asked.

"Yes, you will write quite a few books" was the astounding answer.

"But I only want to write this one as I feel so strongly about it". I replied stubbornly, I didn't intend becoming an author, I just wanted to get this all off my chest, about ghosts and their confusion etc.

"You have a new spirit guide, who will help you write, he's African. If you feel hot when you are writing, don't be alarmed, just know that he is close."

Well, was I freaked out or what? I only wanted to express myself, not take dictation from spirit guides. So onto my next point, I still had a question about my business deal.

"You know my business deal, well it's going so well, are you influencing Mrs Fellows?" I asked hesitantly, sort of wanting to know but also wanting to credit myself with all the skill in pulling off the deal on my own.

"If we want you to do our work, we want to be sure you can eat" came the answer. So yes they were influencing things but I still played my part. They were not telling me or the other party what to do, each was operating from their own intuition or inspiration but probably with a little help and guidance.

Whilst writing this book I have realised that there are other subjects I would like to write about – ideas that are not really appropriate to include here. So I do feel more willing to accept the spirit guides idea that I may write loads of books.

Another experience that was helpful involved slightly more direct intervention than just the influence of my intuition.

Imagine a young lad, quite romantic but not actually in love. He finds physical compatibility with a particular girl, both recognising that their hearts were not really for each other. So this young man has his affair and sometimes bestows his romantic favours on the relationship.

Once when I took this girl, who I'll call Angie, out for a meal in Berkhamsted. We had a fabulous evening with flowers on the table, champagne, great food and exquisite service. We laughed and frankly it was a perfect evening. We took a further bottle of champagne and headed back to my dream, fairy-tale cottage in the country. Both of us were cuddling and expressing love and romance, intending to light the open fire and express our feelings more fully.

Now this Angie, a lovely girl, is pretty clairvoyant with several experiences of seeing her mother who died a while back. She had also seen a pilot friend, after his death, who had always said that he couldn't see his future beyond thirty, then he died, at thirty.

The champagne was flowing and I was busy crouched by the fire looking forward to the rest of the evening when Angie suddenly said.

"There's a man in that chair" she said.

"Don't worry, he won't hurt you whoever he is." My usual confident belief that spirits and ghosts are innately good showing through, even after the champagne.

"Well, I'm going to the loo." And off she went up to the bathroom. I wasn't that impressed at the intrusion, I mean who needs that when... you know?

Down came Angie, looking even less impressed than I was.

"I've just been sick. I felt great, but when I got to the bathroom and opened the door I just had to throw up."

No wonder she didn't look pleased. We chatted, she felt fine now. The man in the chair had gone, but so had our romantic mood.

We went upstairs to sleep, without the romantic magic we'd created: we were back down to earth.

"So what?" I can hear you saying. "The girl had just drank too much alcohol and was sick – happened to me loads of times."

Well, the following Monday I went round for the usual regular sitting and unusually my Dad, came through. He rarely comes and I don't ask him to. I accept he's got his own life to lead on the other side and I don't need to interrupt his life when I can speak to other guiding spirits more appropriately assigned to supporting my life.

Anyway, my Dad came through and then the penny dropped. I could sense this mood of, I call it, sheepishness. A sort of cheeky guilt or embarrassment filled the atmosphere of the room.

"Yes" he confessed it was him who was in the chair, he made Angie sick.

"Thanks Dad." I said smiling, I now understood the importance of breaking the magic of that moment. How inappropriate it would have been and how intoxicating an experience it would have been for both

Angie and me, perhaps leading us to believe there was more to our relationship than there really was.

The Spiritual help or influence available, is not always what you'd expect or ask for, but the value is definitely there. If you consider this example with my Dad, if I hadn't gone to the seance or if Angie hadn't been able to see clairvoyantly she may still have been made sick and the value of the intervention would have existed. The value would have still occurred but I wouldn't have known about it and may have simply concluded that the girl drank too much.

How many experiences like that are we all totally unaware of? How often have you been surprised at the 'turn of events'? Where most unlikely or unexpected outcomes have manifested right before your eyes?

Solicitors can be inspired

When I was offered the chance to buy a Franchise in the estate agency company I worked for, I was enthusiastic – it really seemed an unbelievable opportunity, almost too good to be true.

The deal was agreed in principle and as I awaited the draft Franchise Agreement I recognised the need for 'independent' legal advice.

I highlight 'independent' because estate agents know many solicitors and have pretty good relations with most of them. My boss knew many of them and he understandably carried considerably more weight with them than I did, at just 23.

In my search for a Lawyer I consulted the spirit people, at the regular circle. When I was invited to ask questions after the usual Rescue session, I asked about selecting a solicitor. I was planning to seek one in a particular town where my employer had as few contacts as I did, so there would be little chance of conflicting interests.

The spirit people confirmed that this town would indeed offer the right Solicitor and that I should pick one with an 'R' from Yellow Pages.

A bit vague, I thought, but a help none the less.

So, a firm with an 'R' at the beginning of their title was found as nominated firm and a man, who I shall refer to as Mr. Johnson became the person responsible for my transaction.

Johnson was quick witted and a skillful negotiator. He knew when to push an issue and when to advise me to acquiesce. He was confident of his Law and his own ability. My boss who was selling the franchise chose a firm with a bigger and smarter reception area than the office I was buying!

Johnson turned out to be a well inspired choice, he was always quick to suggest we all get round the table to reach agreement by discussion rather than slow and costly waves of correspondence. He was so confident of his knowledge of the file that he was not intimidated by a larger firm of lawyers.

In short, this man was ideal for the job. What was even better, he did not delegate the file to an assistant, he actually handled the matter himself and knew the transaction so intimately that mistakes caused by delegation were eliminated.

Anyway, negotiations went well, I got the agreement changed to my entire satisfaction and was delighted with the choice of Solicitor.

It turned out that Johnson, was quite spiritually enlightened himself. I didn't mention my spiritual interests for ages, so neither did he. When we finally covered that subject, after negotiations were concluded, Johnson told me of his Spiritual Healing and how he used Pendulum Dowsing when he wanted further confirmation on a matter.

Now how about that? I get a brilliant solicitor who, when he's had clients in his office, has been known to say, "Hang on. Does your shoulder sort of hurt just here?" Pointing to his own body as he spoke. When the client, there for legal counselling remember, replies in the affirmative, Johnson gets up and walks round behind the clients chair and lays his hands on them to give Healing.

Who knows what the Law Society will make of this? I suppose they'll worry that his insurance indemnity doesn't cover such things.

But how good is that? I discover a really psychically aware solicitor, I think it's wonderful and he gets a client who shares the same philosophy.

The use of a pendulum is a brilliant way of accessing information and it works for everyone. Basically you have an object on the end of a thread, free to swing. The swings vary in accordance with questions asked and many people use this as a way of obtaining answers. You don't have to be psychic and it doesn't matter whether you believe that it is

Spiritually operated or operated by you through your unconscious, the pendulum will swing to give yes or no answers. That's what Johnson would use it for, when he was slightly unsure of his next move. More on Pendulums later.

A further aside regarding the franchise acquisition. At the time I bought the franchise, the business was led by a very dynamic and 'gifted' man. I respected this man immensely and still do. I was quite happy to be a part of his group of companies but was not willing to agree to those parts of the Franchise Agreement that would enable my boss, who I respect, to sell his company and I would remain in a Franchise where the owner may be less worthy of respect.

Even though the furthest thing from our minds, at the time, was the boss selling his interest in the 'parent' company of all the Franchises, I was not willing to proceed unless I established some protection against "the old man" selling out.

I knew I would be quite happy to pay a percentage of my business turnover to someone I respected but I wanted to be able to get out of the franchise rather than pay money to someone I didn't like.

Eventually such an assurance was established through a side agreement. Johnson assisted with the negotiations and expressed my resolution that this was essential and how it was really a vote of confidence for my boss. The side letter was agreed.

With the benefit of hindsight, I feel that between Johnson and myself, we were psychically inspired to pursue that side letter with such determination because within six years the company was sold to an insurance company.

Big Help from the Spirit People

A great example of the influence of the spirit world on our lives

are the events surrounding my friends' house sale. The friends, Tony and Patricia are the couple who I used to have the regular seances with and over the years they've had many examples of predictions, which seemed impossible, actually coming true. This one may have been important as the spirit people may have wanted them to move to a place suited to their future Rescue work.

There was the time when they were told by the spirit people that Tony would be offered redundancy and it took so long that it seemed impossible, then he got it and they went to find a guest house and set up their own business.

When they found their dream hotel on the coast they couldn't really believe that they'd be able to buy it as they hadn't sold their own house, which would be essential for providing the funds. The vendor of the Hotel was in a great rush to sell and this seemed to make the whole thing even less likely to Tony and Patricia.

So here we begin to follow the events. Tony and Patricia came back from the coast very excited and held a seance. Yes, the spirit people confirmed that they had indeed found the right Hotel and confirmed the price to offer. They also said that Tony and Patricia would move to that Hotel.

I was an Estate Agent in the town where Tony and Patricia lived and it seemed only natural, as I sat at a seance with them, that they entrust me with the sale of their house. We duly got the house on the market and we awaited spectacular results, for if they were to get their hotel, surely they'd need a cash buyer immediately.

The house was duly placed on the market and attracted good attention being excellent accommodation. The third person to view was a young man. His parents had both died recently and he had a brother to look after with a reasonable inheritance to help provide for both of their futures. We'll call him Stephen.

Yes, Stephen wanted the house. It would suit him well. It was large enough for him and his brother to share and still have their own environments. It was near the station and town centre so they need not be too dependent on cars or public transport.

Yes, Stephen would have the house. He actually said as he viewed "I will buy your house". He consulted my Estate Agent's office and the finance seemed really straightforward – he had money in trust with one of the big Clearing Banks. The Estate Agency could recommend him as a qualified buyer.

At a seance we asked about Stephen. He seemed so young, would he really buy their house? "YES" came the answer, no messing, the spirit people were very positive about this.

The wheels began slowly turning. The Estate Agents wrote letters confirming the sale and Solicitors were instructed to begin preparing the contract of sale.

Then things started going so slowly that they almost stopped. The bank trustees just would not appreciate the urgency or respond to Stephen's requests for rapid action. Stephen, who wanted the house, told them to hurry up but they were so slow and maybe they thought he was too young and they just failed to respond. Until Stephen was older the Bank Trustees had to approve this sort of decision so his hands were tied, he could only wait.

The house remained on the market and many people, now considered sightseers by Tony and Patricia, continued to view.

No cash buyer came. Many people viewed the renovated and well decorated, three story Victorian semi but no offers were forthcoming.

More and more people viewed. It was uncanny. At the time we expected that if ten people viewed a house one of them would buy or at least make an offer. Nothing.

My friends were becoming more anxious about their move. At a seance I heard them ask again and be told that yes they would be buying that hotel. Yes, their house would sell.

Tony said "I'll believe it when I see it", chuckling to himself. After all his experiences he still finds it incredible the things that the spirit people can arrange but here the odds just seemed so heavily stacked against the prediction coming true.

"Should we drop the price of our house?" Tony asked. No! The spirit people were emphatic, the house will sell.

More people viewed. Over ninety people viewed that house before they moved. They thought theirs was a stately home and were wondering if they should start charging admission.

Still no progress, no other offers.

"Yes" the spirit people said, "you will buy the Hotel and Stephen will buy your house".

Stephen did have a house already that went onto the market, but having been occupied by young lads it was not always presented at its tidiest and didn't sell.

The bank trustees were to provide a bridging loan urgently so Stephen could buy the house.

Eventually the bank said it wasn't that happy about the house being

Victorian – they were not keen on such an old house.

The Estate Agent suggested a Structural Survey to satisfy the Bank. The house had been well renovated by Mr Smith since he bought it in 1969. The first time I went round to their house Tony was under the floorboards in the kitchen doing something, I think to the wiring.

So a surveyor was instructed and he carried out his inspection between appointments for more viewers. The number of viewers was up in the seventies now, the number of people who hadn't viewed was becoming less than those who had!

A copy of the survey report was dispatched to the bank. We all waited with baited breath. Nothing, the bank said nothing.

Another buyer appeared miraculously. One of the viewers, a bank employee being transferred wanted the house for his large family. Coming from the north of England, where prices were lower, he had a large detached house but he recognised there was enough room although the house was a semi.

His offer was acceptable and he was invited to proceed with the purchase. Tony and Patricia had virtually given up with Stephen, but they asked the Estate Agent to tell him of the other buyer.

Stephen's bank trustees had read the survey and still were not that keen on him bridging on such a mature house, even though the report only raised minor items which Stephen was completely happy about.

All seemed lost for Stephen, even the Estate Agents felt sure that the Bank Employee would get the house.

"Yes, you will buy the hotel and Stephen will buy your house". The spirit people were still adamant that Stephen would get it.

The negotiations with the owner of the Hotel on the coast were ok, but he was becoming anxious about the length of time the Smiths were taking to sign the contract to buy.

Actually visiting Tony and Patricia for the circle every week during this protracted transaction was enjoyable, but for the slow progress with their house sale. They were brilliant about the delays but, as the owner of the Estate Agency office, I was quite embarrassed about the length of time it was all taking and was finding it hard to believe that the spirit people were right this time.

It was quite odd for me though, as I worked at another Estate office, I used to get updates from my colleagues at the local and would regularly hear how well things were going for the bank employee. But I would have an inner knowledge that Stephen was going to buy the house in spite of what I was told.

Eventually, to cut a fourteen month long story short, Stephen did suddenly sort out his trustees, the trustee actually came himself to see the house and the deal went through with Stephen almost immediately afterwards. The Bank employee was disappointed but as efficient and honest Estate Agents, we had told him of the full circumstances. I had not however told the Estate Agent of the weight of the spirit effort that was behind Stephen buying the house.

To me, this whole episode was a major example of the intricate nature of the spirits' guidance of our lives. They particularly wanted Stephen to have the house. He was very gifted psychically and as the house had been used as a 'channel' for spirits recently passed over into the spirit world, they wanted some continuity for the house.

This is just one example where spiritual values are influencing our lives. It just happens that with this house move I was aware of the likely outcome that suited the spirit people. I also believe that in many house moves or any major transaction there will be spiritual factors considered and influencing the outcome. I bet you can think of at least one incident where a beneficial outcome resulted, against the odds.

The outcome would have been the same even without the inside knowledge being available. For example, even though the Smiths were told that Stephen would get the house, they still rationally agreed to sell to the bank employee as it seemed so unlikely that Stephen would ever buy the house. Tony and Patricia did not try to influence events to suit the spirit prediction.

Buying my house

As a young ambitious estate agent I'd bought a cottage and renovated it. The house prices and my salary had risen to such an extent that I felt under mortgaged and wanted to move to a more expensive house and move back into the town from the country where my cottage was.

I spotted a great little house to buy in a road called Park Hill. A super late Victorian cottage, almost a small villa style with three bedrooms, one of which could be converted to accommodate a bathroom.

Ideal for me, I thought. Having had experience of renovating a cottage I was confident that I could do this within my budget and have quite a good buy. Very excited, I submitted my offer to the estate agent down the road from my own office, and waited for the answer.

In the meantime at the regular circle, I asked if I would buy the house in Park Hill. Yes, the spirit people said without hesitation.

The reply to my offer however was that I was too low. There was someone else interested. The next offer I made was higher, really at my upper financial limit. Again I waited for the answer from the agent, quite confident that my offer would be accepted, because the spirit people had been positive, I was going to buy Park Hill.

No, The other offer was accepted, they were selling to the other interested party. The agent was a highly ethical man, who I will always respect, so I knew there was no changing his mind. In fact he laughed, "It's funny when you think how often you have had to disappoint purchasers, it's funny that it should happen to you".

I shared his joke as best I could but was still wondering how the spirit people had been so wrong. "Perhaps the deal will fall through and I will buy the house after all", I wondered.

I just waited to see what would happen. Eventually my impatience got the better of me and one morning I dropped in on the Estate Agent to ask how the sale was proceeding.

"Fine Lance, but I do have this house that is just going onto the market, it may suit you even better than the other one" was the news from the Agent.

Incredibly the house was within my price, needed updating, had space to extend and was in Park Hill. It was much more suitable than the other one and in the same road. I was beginning to realise that the spirit people had perhaps known of this house and this was the one they meant when they said I'd buy in Park Hill.

I borrowed the key to the house. It was empty and I rushed up to view it. Ideal, for only a bit more work and investment this would be a four bedroom two bathroom house. Driving back to return the key I saw a friend of mine who does all the surveys locally for a major building society.

"Come with me" I said as I lured my surveyor pal to Park Hill to see the house. He noted that work was required but told me he would recommend it as a sound security for a mortgage to his Building Society so long as the work was done, if he carried out an official survey.

In the light of his advice, knowing I had an account with the Building Society he surveyed for and that I would qualify for a mortgage from them, already being an investor with the local branch, I was confident that I could buy this house.

When I returned the key, within an hour of borrowing it, I made an offer of the asking price and told the agent that I'd already had my Building Society survey done, for in a sense I had.

The sale was duly agreed and proceeded smoothly. I did get the meaning of the spirit people's prediction – this was the house they had in mind for me all along.

This demonstrated to me that it is important to follow the advice and predictions without interpretation, even when they seem really unlikely.

Perhaps they encouraged my surveyor friend to be in my path to assist my purchase. Perhaps the first house I lost got me more ready to buy and to recognise the need to act rapidly when the right house came up.

Whatever the reason for what happened, I was very happy with the house and enjoyed my time there. Losing the first house did improve my ability as an Estate Agent, made me more sympathetic to purchasers when things didn't work out for them, so I value that experience too.

Our Sense of knowing

Quite often in a lifetime we have an experience that demonstrates our own psychic or intuitive abilities. The experience may be personal and hard to describe to others, for fear of being thought crazy or ridiculous.

When talking with Gill, a good friend, the subject of ghosts and spirits came up. After some intense conversation Gill began to share her experiences that demonstrated to her that there was more to life than met the eye.

Gill was delighted to have someone to talk to at last, when we got chatting, the other day. She found that she just couldn't talk to people about her psychic experiences. "What if people think I'm weird?"

How many of us are like Gill? Since I became more open about my views and beliefs it has amazed me how many of my friends and acquaintances are similarly minded and have longed to speak to someone about "something funny that happened to me". They thought no one would understand.

Gill was able to share her stories with someone at last and they illustrate a point about our deeper sense of knowing. How we somehow know more about each other than we allow ourselves to be aware of consciously.

Gill's experience took place when she was travelling down through France in the back of her parent's car with her family, over ten years ago. She was 13 years old, and looking forward to the camping holiday with her younger brother and her parents.

During the journey, about half way through France to their destination Gill caught her parent's attention.

"We've got to go back. It's Grandad, he's not well." Gill said, for no apparent reason.

"Don't worry, you've been dreaming" her parents rationalised, as we probably all would with such alarmist news coming from a child.

At the camp site the parents received the news. Grandad had been taken seriously ill. Doctors thought he would surely die at any moment, but he seemed to just keep hanging on.

They hadn't left their holiday address so it was a miracle that the news reached them at all. But they were even more confused by their daughter's startling revelation on the journey.

Gill's mother flew back to see Grandad in hospital; he didn't really acknowledge that she was there, but he seemed to relax and just passed away quite peacefully.

They never solved the mystery of the daughter's 'sense of knowing' about her Grandad's death. The family stopped talking about it and Gill was left wondering for a long time, unable to mention it really. Who would believe her or understand?

Gill was also pleased to talk about the time she saw her Grandfather, at least she thinks it must have been him. Gill came home one day to the family house. Her parents were out but her brother was at home.

Gill wandered around the house doing the usual sort of things when she saw a man walking down the hall into the kitchen. It was so real that she thought there was indeed someone, who she didn't immediately recognise, in the house. She called her brother, "Have you got any friends here?"

"No," her brother answered. So the house was empty apart from the two of them. Gill searched the house. Her image had been so 'real' that she couldn't believe it herself. There just had to be someone else in the house.

No, the house was empty apart from her brother and it definitely wasn't him that she saw.

Eventually Gill accepted that this was some ghost she'd seen. She rationalised her vision and assumed that it was her recently deceased Grandfather.

So here's Gill, a gifted visionary who is discouraged by our society from talking about her experience or given no obvious direction to develop or enhance those psychic skills.

I am constantly amazed by the number of people busting to talk about ghosts and the like. Just about everyone I meet, knows someone who had 'a funny experience'. Well, why don't we agree now that it is ok to talk about it, that there is nothing wrong with psychic phenomena, nothing to be afraid of or embarrassed about. That there is nothing evil to be feared as the church has been trying to convince us all for years. Let's talk about it. I think we'll all be amazed at how common these psychic events are and as we become more accepting of them so they'll occur more and become more useful and easily directed.

Our whole lives and consciousness could expand as a direct result of being more open to discussion and to our own psychicness.

Eighteen

SPIRITUAL HEALING

No book on ghosts and spirits would be complete without some mention of the amazing work done through spirits that can be so beneficial to our health. While you are reading with such an open mind I would just like to share a few ideas with you.

There are many books (listed in the Bibliography) on the subject of Spirit Healing giving awe-inspiring stories of Cancer cures, back injuries being spirited away at a touch. Also there is an address for those people wanting to receive healing and for those who wish to train as healers.

There are two stories I will share, as I know the people involved well enough to be sure of the accuracy of the account.

Tony's mother was a very gifted psychic and healer. When I had a session with her I hardly had the chance to speak to her, she went into trance so quickly. She sat in her chair and immediately went off into trance and Jacob, one of her spirit guides, came through straight away. It was so quick and simple and Jacob just chatted to me, dealing with issues that only I could know about and giving sagacious comments.

Between them, having a session with Tony's mum and Jacob was a formidable experience. There are other mediums in London, and I'm sure, all over the world who operate in such a quick and confident manner. Well worth a visit though, if you don't mind discovering that some spirits seem to know more about you than you know yourself.

Tony's mum was well known in the Devonshire village where the family lived. She was often consulted and asked for a reading or for healing. Her family had been 'at it' for years. Later when they moved to Bedfordshire her two boys were in a serious car accident. I will let Tony tell his story in his own words:

In September 1959 I decided to travel to work with my brother in his car.

It was a Heinkel bubble car, only six months old. We left home at 6.45 am, travelling from Bletchley to Luton. Approaching Hockliffe village on the A5, suddenly the car swerved across the road into the path of an oncoming timber lorry. Our car hit the lorry's front wheel and on impact the car was struck with such force as to turn it to face the opposite direction. The only thought in my mind was that I would not come out of this alive. I was thrown through the windscreen and landed very heavily on my back in the road. My brother was still in the car and received serious facial injuries.

We were taken to Luton and Dunstable hospital. I had lacerated the nerves in my right wrist, necessitating emergency surgery. I was very lucky that the surgeon who was on duty that day had been studying my type of injury. I was told that I would have only limited use of my hand due to the extent of the damage and the type of repair that had to be carried out.

Because of the injury to my back I was unable to walk at first. the surgeon told me that when I could walk the length of the ward I could go home.

I struggled after 10 days to walk that ward. The sweat was pouring off me, but my only thought was to get home so that I could have spirit healing. Because of his injury my brother was transferred to Mount Vernon hospital for plastic surgery.

When I was receiving healing the spirit guide told me that my brother would be looked after and helped.

My arm was in plaster at this time. When the plaster was eventually removed the surgeon who treated me in the first place seemed genuinely surprised at the way my arm had healed up. It had healed extremely well and very quickly. Instead of being useless I could almost make a fist, even in those early days.

After much help from my spirit friends, and rehabilitation at work I now have full use of my hand. The only thing that is not quite right is, that I have no sensation nerves. Therefore, I do not feel the first pain the same as everyone else. I do not withdraw my hand instinctively from heat or cold. I only feel sharp pain.

When you consider that in 1959 microsurgery was not on the medical agenda, I feel that without the help of the healing that was received at that time, my hand would not be as good today as it is.

As for my brother, he had several operations to repair the damage to his face. Today he has virtually no scarring and little or no after-effects.

How complete was Tony's cure? Pretty incredible, he's been working with his hands all his life as a maintenance engineer and the only problem he has with that hand is that he doesn't always know if he hurts it.

When you see the scars and consider the Doctor's original prognosis, not being aware of pain is nothing when you consider he may have lost all use of the hand.

Another example, from the same family coincidentally, involves Tony's daughter Sally.

Sally, at 10 months old, was playing, crawling in the kitchen while her mother was cooking. Where they lived the kitchen was a step down from the breakfast area, quite common in Victorian houses where the old scullery is converted into living space.

Sally in an effort to get up to tackle the step, placed her hand with all her little weight, with the intention of pushing herself up, on the door of the oven. You know the sort of oven with a door that opens down so you can lift the roast out onto it for basting.

The oven door was scorching, having just been opened, and Sally's hand was dreadfully burnt. A trip to hospital for treatment with the Doctors concluding that she'd be scarred for life and may lose her sense of feeling in the palm of her hand.

The parents were still of the same faith as Tony's mum had always been and they prayed that Sally would be healed with no disability or scarring. You can imagine how bad they felt about leaving the oven door open and hurting their little baby.

Sally's cot was in a bedroom with her slightly older sister and as usual that night the children went to bed.

The parents were used to sitting at a seance and they decided they'd sit that night to request help for Sally, they were very worried about her and wanted to do all they could for her.

They sat and the usual guides came through and told them that Sally would be all right. "There's a Doctor here to see her" they were told. For this family it seemed quite normal for a Spirit Doctor to visit their daughter and they had some comfort and peace of mind.

The next day at breakfast the family was downstairs when suddenly the older daughter Carol said, as if she suddenly remembered to ask:

"Who was that man with Sally last night?"

The parents were fascinated but not that surprised and simply encouraged Carol to elaborate by asking "Who do you mean? What did he look like?"

Carol described how a man in a white coat had come into the room and looked at Sally's hand, then had just gone away.

The family felt much better and looked forward to the dressings being taken off. Yes, you guessed, no scars, no loss of any senses it was a perfectly healed injury. I've seen these hands and you wouldn't even know which one was burnt in the first place.

A Spiritual insight into a medical cure

This is an example from my own experience where the spirit people were able to encourage me to seek the best medical treatment.

In a Show House, when a prospective buyer wants to look out of the window, if you're the site representative, you open the window. Unfortunately, I was the site representative and the window had been painted with gloss paint and closed while the paint was still wet. It seemed stuck fast. I thought that a gentle tap with the fist should fix it and may even go unnoticed by the prospective purchaser.

Yes, the tap with the knuckles worked a treat, the window was open, "what a lovely view".

The trouble was, my wrist hurt like hell. Not only had the sudden but quite slight impact jarred the grip of the dried paint, it had also jarred my wrist. It felt all hot and sore, burning inside like a trapped nerve.

After a few days my wrist seemed to only hurt in certain positions so I assumed it was getting better.

Three weeks after the injury I was becoming annoyed with the pain when I moved my wrist and wanted healing to progress faster than this. It really did hurt.

At the regular circle I was attending, there came a time when I was invited to ask a question. This usually only happens when I do have a question that I'm very keen to ask.

"What about my wrist, should I see the Doctor?" I asked the spirit people.

There was a pause in the proceedings, not uncommon when this sort of question is asked. It seems to me that the spirit people call up a spirit Doctor and he has a quick look at the part in question then shares his diagnosis, which is passed on via the other spirit guides.

The funniest example of this was with the dog who used to be in the lounge where we held the seances. He'd be asleep in front of the gas fire, not at all bothered about what we were doing. The family may have been worried about their dog and would ask about his chest injury or his bad paw. Nearly always injuries incurred through his enthusiasm or his inability to believe that other dogs wanted to bite him, he was so loving.

They would ask about the dog at the seance, there would be the usual pause and then the funny thing; the dog would sort of lift his head up and move around a bit, looking confused as if he really was being examined by an invisible vet. This was quite extraordinary to see.

Then the guides would share the vet's diagnosis and the dog would simply go back to sleep now he wasn't being prodded about.

With my wrist, the spirit people said I needed to see the Doctor and a specialist at the City hospital. "See the Doctor first and do what he says but the Specialist will fix it, we can inspire him." The spirit people gave their answer and I followed their instructions.

The Doctor suggested rest and sent me to a local hospital to get a wrist support to restrict movement giving the tendon a chance to recover.

A few weeks later, as agreed, I went back to the Doctor who noted the lack of progress. "Let's try ultrasound, it's a bit like black magic, but sometimes it works".

I went back to the local hospital and handed in the note from my Doctor. The physiotherapist gave me a course of treatment including hot wax on my wrist and holding a machine that projected ultrasonic vibrations into my wrist. I can't remember how long this went on but it did no good. I didn't notice any decrease in pain when I moved my wrist. By now I was naturally enough learning which positions not to move my wrist into, so there was less often pain but it still hurt like hell when I forgot and used my wrist normally.

During all these treatments the message at the seance was the same, "you'll be ok when you see the specialist at the City Hospital".

Knowing that the answer lay with a specialist I waited with patience for my own Doctor to give up on the 'black magic' of the local hospital and refer me to the City.

Finally, the Doctor gave up on my wrist and referred me to the specialist named by the spirit people. Elated and relieved I took the first available appointment with the specialist and arrived early so as not to miss my turn. I think I had only to wait about a week but it seemed much longer as I was so keen to see this chap I'd heard about from the Spirit people and who was going to bring relief to my disabled wrist.

Within ten minutes I was out of the hospital having had an injection of cortisone 'up the tendon' and I was on the road to recovery. When the specialist said "Now this really could hurt quite a bit", before giving the injection, I wasn't at all concerned. The spirit people could inspire this man so I had complete faith in his ability and the injection hardly hurt at all.

My wrist was back to normal within two weeks, thankfully.

The process of getting treatment was just as protracted as it would have been without the information from the seance, but having that information really was a comfort and gave me greater patience. I now trust though that with the medical profession I will always see Doctors, nurses and specialists who are as easily inspired to do what is right for me. I therefore seldom feel the need to seek out the spiritual guidance as I did with my wrist.

Whilst some see Spiritual Healing and Holistic medicine as 'alternative medicine' I do think we should recognise that many medical practitioners are spiritually influenced and inspired. This can mean that you will receive both traditional medicine and at the same time have spiritual healing without Doctor or patient being aware of the alternative therapy being administered.

There is a whole world of information and belief about health and I recommend further reading in this area. See the Bibliography and you will find books that explore why we get ill and what to do about it.

Paul the Healer – Ray the Medium

Of the healers I have met, the most remarkable is a man called Ray Brown. He works in a way which is interesting to watch and very effective. I know this because I have seen him heal others and had the benefit of healing from him.

When Ray is healing, he is in full trance and not aware of the work being done through him. This is possible because he is a full trance medium and the spirit he works with, Paul, takes him over completely to do his work.

Paul, the actual spirit who does the work, was a Judaen physician who lived at the time of Christ and travelled with the Roman armies doing surgery on their battle wounds.

Paul has been preparing Ray for this work for over twenty years and only relatively recently has ray taken the brave step to commit all his time to healing by giving up his normal job.

Ray and Paul are two very different characters and their attitudes to each other is rather amusing. Ray wears glasses which Paul immediately takes off when he is using Ray's body "I can't see through these" is Paul's attitude to spectacles.

Ray is a relatively shy individual, who first encountered spirit healing at 15, he worked with the very famous healer, Harry Edwards at the age of 16. Paul on the other hand is quite confident and outgoing and handles the work of healing with humour and kindness.

In addition to the work as a healer, Paul gives talks to groups on many aspects of our lives and the nature of his home environment in the spirit world.

These talks are most impressive and enlightening. Paul brings humour to the proceedings and often includes a demonstration of his healing abilities.

The details of the different planes of existence in the spirit world is all rather confusing and hard for us mortals to understand. He advises on how to live healthily and shares his belief that healing environments should be cheerful places and where happiness is encouraged and stimulated.

Paul is a spirit of remarkable healing ability. There are so many cases where his therapy has been extremely and almost immediately effective that there are too many to mention here.

Paul describes himself as a pioneer in the work of spirit in psychic operations on our bodies. When he performs his operations on patients it involves his spirit hands passing from those of the medium into the flesh of the patient. The ability to do this is only a recent development which he has achieved. This skill allows him to manipulate parts of the body internally that would normally only be accessible with normal surgery, for example releasing trapped nerves.

Spirit healing used to be performed by laying on of hands or by holding the healers hands just a few inches from the patient. The ability for the spirit hands to work inside the body of a patient is a remarkable breakthrough for both our material world and, according to Paul, the spirit side as well.

Paul's work includes training a team of Doctor on the spirit side to work in the same way he does with Ray and he hopes to see this type of healing become more acceptable and available within our normal health service.

One of the big differences between a treatment from Paul and other healers is his diagnostic ability. Because Ray is in trance and allows Paul to communicate fully with the patient, Paul can look inside the patient, see the difficulty, do his stuff and tell the patient how they are. He can give a prognosis, not usually available from a healer in the same detail.

A friend of mine Beth, went to see Paul, because some of her fingers had become very swollen and sore at the middle joint to the extent that she could hardly use her hands. After one month off sick from work and all sorts of tests from the NHS Doctor including one for rheumatoid arthritis, which proved negative, Paul was worth a try.

On hearing that the problem was with three fingers on each hand, the little fingers and thumbs were not troubled, Paul gave his diagnosis.

"In that case it must be a trapped nerve just here." and he put his (Ray's) hand on the back of the girl's neck.

"Yes, here it is". He could see the nerve and began to free it. The patient felt a ping of discomfort as the nerve was freed. Paul worked down each of the patients arms in turn, massaging the nerve that had been pinched in the neck.

He eased the nerve all the way down to the fingers on each hand. Within a week the girl had her finger movement back, unimpeded and the swelling had gone.

Beth visited her Doctor and explained the healing that she had received from Paul. The Doctor seemed totally at ease and relaxed and was delighted to hear that the girl no longer had the complaint. Beth was encouraged to find that at least one doctor was open to this new way of being healed.

To meet Paul is quite incredible. Often when I go to see him, for healing or when I take someone else, I'll say, "Hello Paul, how are you?"

And he'll answer "I'm ok, I'm dead. It's you people that have all the problems."

Paul has a quick wit and a good sense of humour and is well known for his joke about having been sent back to work with someone as 'dumb' as Ray, as a punishment. He also jokes that he must have been a terrible surgeon because he only gets a rusty bike to come back to the Earth plane on.

Ray jokes about Paul and sometimes even calls Paul, 'The Skirt' because of the Roman clothes that he wears. Their banter is amusing and helps people relax and enjoy the experience rather than be perturbed by what is going on.

Paul has been known, when treating patients with a stomach problem, as he examines them and looks inside to say, for example, "Oh fish and chips, the first time I've seen them" thus describing the contents of the stomach and the lunch the patient has just eaten!

Most patients who visit Ray (or should I say Paul?) for treatment only see Paul, because Ray spends most of the day for the clinic in full trance. He will only come out of trance for his lunch, so most patients don't see the striking difference in mannerism and conversation between the two people using the one body.

Paul advocates relaxation and visualisation as a necessary part of our lives to deal with the stresses of our society. To this end he has made a wonderful relaxation cassette, which helps those who use it to maintain a healthy body and a calm mind. The tape is similar to a hypnotherapy or relaxation tape but Paul's message, coming from spirit, is rather special.

Incidentally, even though Ray and Paul use the same vocal chords, their voices are quite different.

A contact address for Ray Brown is given at the end of the book.

Nineteen

PENDULUM DOWSING

Now whatever you believe so far this will work for you even if you don't really believe in all this stuff, unless you really don't want it to succeed.

A pendulum can be used to answer any question you ask where yes or no can be the answer. Holding it by the string, from the direction of the swing of the pendulum, you can determine the answer. This is a valuable method for obtaining additional advice to help with decision making. The decision either comes from an unconscious movement or a movement inspired spiritually. One of the benefits of this is that it can satisfy the curiosity of those who may be wanting the information they feel they may get from a spirit at a circle.

Now before I get into how you program yourself and the pendulum to give the three different swings, yes, no or I don't know, I will just make one or two comments (while I've got your attention).

When I show people how I use my pendulum, I show the three different swings or else I ask a question and show the pendulum swing to give my yes or no answer. Do you know what they say? They say "But you moved it, I saw you".

"Yes, of course I move the pendulum." How else could it possibly move? They seem to want to fix it to some solid object and see it move on its own!

However, whilst I know I must be moving it, I am not conscious of moving it. It will move to give an answer even if I'm not watching it and I don't consciously know what answer it will give, even if I have a consciously preferred answer.

One of two things happens; either it's psychic and my spirit or my spirit guides make me move to swing the pendulum I'm holding or my unconscious says yes or no with the pendulum to state its, or my unconscious', preference.

Anyway, who cares how it works if it does and it's useful and fun. Let's leave the reasoning to scientists and get on with the exercise.

How do you start to use a pendulum?

Well take anything small, I used a car key because it already had a bit of string on it, attach a piece of light string or cotton to it about ten inches (25cm) long.

Hold the string of the pendulum about half way up between your finger and thumb with your finger and thumb pointing downwards. Fig 1.

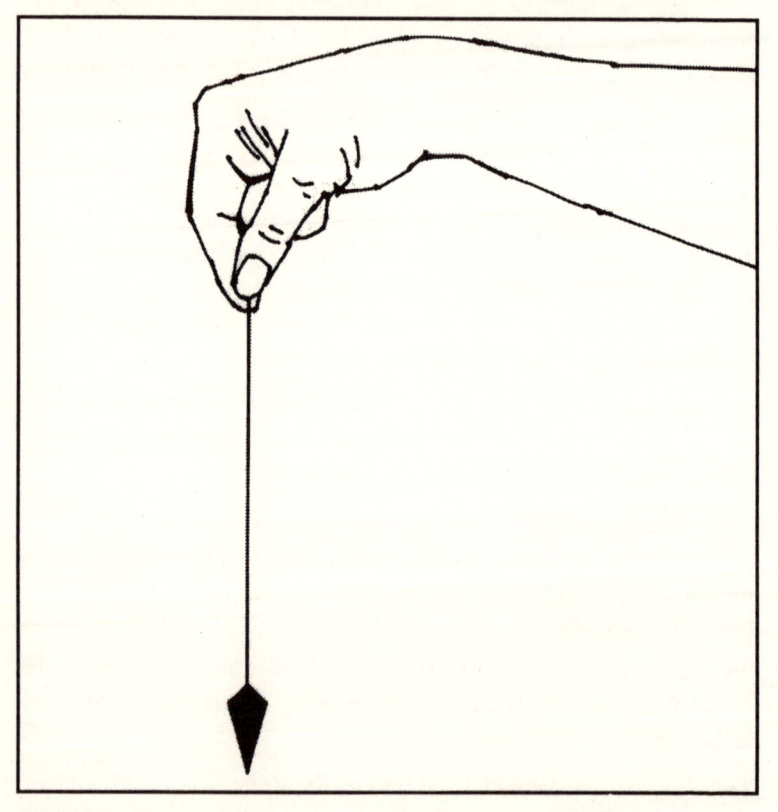

Fig. 1

Now what you are going to do, is sit down in an upright chair and hold the pendulum in two different positions to get two different swings. Look at the picture Fig 2. to see the two likely swings, this is very important, so you know what to look for from the pendulum's movements.

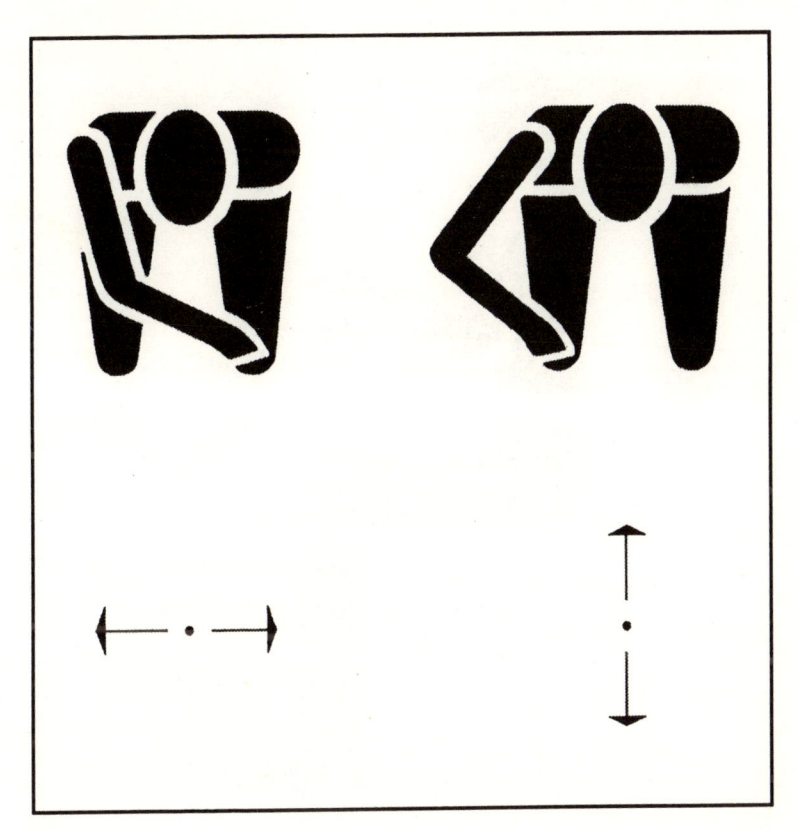

Fig. 2

Now hold the pendulum, for the first swing, over your right knee in your right hand (if you're right handed, if you're left handed hold it in your left hand over your left knee). The pendulum should be about one inch or 3 cm above your knee. Don't worry if your arm gets tired with all the holding of the pendulum but it's very important not to rest your elbow on anything, hold your arm clear of your body. Fig 3.

Then the silly bit, best to do the whole process on your own. Say out loud "Give me a swing".

And wait, the pendulum will swing in either of the directions shown in Fig 2. If it is hesitant say "give me a swing" again. If you find this is still unsuccessful, try saying it again and take your eyes and full concentration off the pendulum. Choose to relax and believe that it will work and that it's ok for it to work. After all, it's just your unconscious, it's not spooky or anything.

Fig. 3

When you establish what this first swing is, move the pendulum, still in the same hand, to be about one inch or 3cm above the other knee.

Say again "give me a swing" and you will get a different swing from the first one. Again if you find hesitance, and you probably won't do the same as you did before, you will be amazed at how the pendulum swings and how you are unaware of moving it.

Now that you have had two separate and identifiable swings of the pendulum it's important to identify which one will be yes and which will be no. You can see from the diagram in Fig 2. which one is my yes and which is my no.

To do this hold the pendulum, at the same height as before, ignore your arm if it's tired, do not support your elbow, and let the pendulum hang directly between your knees, not over either one as it was before.

Now you say, out loud, "Give me a yes", asking for a yes swing. The pendulum will swing in one of the two ways you have experienced and this will be your yes swing.

"Give me a no", repeating the process with the pendulum held exactly as it was to establish your yes swing.

The pendulum will swing in your other way, this is your no.

Play with the pendulum, have some fun asking questions and see the yes and no answers quickly occur through the swing of your pendulum.

Now hold the pendulum between your knees and say "Give me an I don't know". The pendulum will take a different swing from the yes or no. My "I don't know" is an anti-clockwise circle. I don't know what your first two swings will be so I cannot predict your third swing but I know I find the circular swing quick and easy to detect, quite different from my yes or no.

So having set up your pendulum, or programmed yourself through your unconscious you can begin to have fun.

I've gone into a local restaurant a little too light hearted and frivolous, slightly inebriated, not minding what I had to eat. I knew I was hungry but I couldn't be bothered to decide what to eat. Who wants to read the menu when you're having a laugh with friends? So I've whipped out my pendulum, put my finger on the menu and said "Shall I have this?" and moved my finger down the page each time I got a "no" until eventually I got a "yes" and had a lovely swordfish steak.

Incidentally, since then, the restaurant manager now uses a pendulum. He uses the cross and chain that he wears round his neck.

I believe my body must know what is good for me to eat at any given time better than I do consciously, even when I've not had a drop of alcohol.

Other uses for the pendulum? There are loads of them. What about the times when you are agreeing to do something, why not get the pendulum out "Is this what I really want to do?" You'll be amazed at the responses. You may, as a result of getting a yes to a question like that, find that you really do want to do something that you didn't feel that keen about, then you put more effort into whatever it is and hence get more value out of doing it.

Anyway the pendulum is a fun thing. Don't rule your life by it but it does give you a chance to test your true feelings.

If you accept, as I do, that on some level we remember everything we see, hear or feel, but only retain the ability to access what we choose to remember, or think we'll need, then this could be a very powerful tool.

If this is a way of quickly and easily accessing your own data bank of your unconscious then you could use it for all sorts of things. If you have a greater sense of knowing than you realise, why not try to access that awareness in this simple way?

Anyway, have fun with it, I do. And when people say, as they surely will, "But I can see you moving it", just say "Yes, of course".

One thing with the pendulum that never ceases to surprise me is how quickly it will stop swinging. Once you get set up, if you get an answer and then simply say "STOP" it is incredible how quickly and firmly your pendulum adopts a stationary position. Try it.

There's a good book on using a pendulum which is listed in the Bibliography.

Twenty

PEARLY GATES

Since beginning to write this book and share some of the experiences that opened my eyes to these views, much has taken place. The last two years have brought many changes and new discoveries.

In February 1992, I had a flash of inspiration about the Pearly Gates, which has dramatically altered my perspective on many things. I'd like to share that new idea with you.

The rescues described earlier always followed a pattern where a ghost would be encouraged to think of his friends who died before him. Thus he would see them and go to the spirit world.

While sitting in a rescue circle communicating and performing rescues, a new method evolved. The more visually psychic member of the group, Beth, 'saw' a circular shaft of bright white light, shining into the room. This bright light only seemed to appear when we were inviting a ghost to look for his relatives.

A number of ghosts came through and they almost immediately found their way to the spirit world once they saw this bright light. It seemed to offer them an irresistible attraction and through it they found their way to the spirit world.

All we needed to do then when a ghost came through was this:

We asked if they knew where they were, which is a sure way to differentiate between a lost ghost and a spirit guide. Once we found that the communicating entity was a ghost we would say:

"Do you know your condition?"

"No" the ghost would answer.

"Look around the room". We would instruct them. As soon as they looked around the room they would see the bright light and instantly go through it or into it.

As Beth thought of the ghost looking round the room the light would brighten, as if she were the channel for the light. A spirit guide with whom we nearly always communicate when we sit, said

"Keep the light gate open" – referring to Beth working on the light and developing her ability to hold the brightness of it.

The concept of the light 'gate' suddenly struck me. Beth had described it as a bright white light, not like yellow sunlight but a sort of pearly white light.

So here was a 'Pearly Gate' that people go through when they die!!

This seems to explain so much for me. It answers all those burning questions that I've harboured for so long. For example if we die we go to the pearly gates, but if we go as pedestrians, without our cars or horses, we'd only need a single pedestrian gate. There would be no need for a pair of pearly gates as I'd imagined them from my early Religious instruction.

So rather than the plural used to describe the gates meaning a single pair of gates, it would mean that there are lots of light gates. There would be lots of these shafts of pearly light gates to guide us over to the new world of spirit.

Not only did this explain the metaphorical teaching of the Bible, but also those descriptions offered by people who survive near death experiences. They so often talk of a bright white light like a sort of tunnel to pass up. Some even talk of seeing friendly figures within the white light. Some say they feel it is like the light of love.

How wonderful for us that these things should correlate! How wonderful to know that the wisdom of the scriptures is accurate even though we have perhaps missed some of the points, by taking the teachings too literally and not assessed their validity as metaphors.

So there you have it, PEARLY LIGHT GATES. Nice isn't it?

More Bible references

Other references to 'the light' are readily available in ancient teaching. The story of Paul on the road to Damascus is a dramatic example. The New Testament records how Paul actively tried to suppress the early Christian movement through persecution (Galations 1:13-14) until he was converted to Christianity by a visionary encounter with a brilliant light representing the risen Jesus while on the road to Damascus about AD 36 (Galations 1:15-16; Acts 9:1-31; 22; 26). Because of this vision, Paul held that he had met Jesus and became a prominent early Christian leader.

His account of the light is contained in Acts 26:

"I saw a light much brighter than the sun, coming from the sky and shining round me and the men travelling with me. All of us fell to the ground, and I heard a voice say to me in Hebrew, 'Saul, Saul! Why are you persecuting me? You are hurting yourself by hitting back, like an ox kicking against its owner's stick.' 'Who are you, Lord?' I asked. And the Lord answered, 'I am Jesus, whom you persecute.' "

John 8:12 "Jesus spoke to the Pharisees again. 'I am the light of the world,' he said. 'Whoever follows me will have the light of life and will never walk in darkness.' "

1 John 1:5 "Now the message that we have heard from his Son and announce is this: God is light, and there is no darkness at all in him."

1 John 1:7 "But if we live in the light - just as he is in the light - then we have fellowship with one another, and the blood of Jesus, his son, purifies us from every sin."

So it does seem that Jesus and the light are one and the same, therefore the light is the way through which we can pass to the next dimension.

When Jesus talks, in John 14:6, of "being the way, the truth, and the life; no one comes to the Father except by me". I feel he may be explaining that he is the 'light' and it is only through the light that we can transfer to the other dimension.

These correlations in religious thinking are very exciting and it is wonderful to find that everything is correct and has merely been interpreted slightly differently and at times too literally. We should look for light, truth and life, not for Jesus himself. Many people see 'the light' in near death experiences some of whom have led very ordinary lives. You don't have to be a servant of the church or even a regular churchgoer to be allowed to die happily, pass through the light and into the next dimension.

Twenty-One

QUESTION TIME

As I mentioned in the introduction, it is inevitable that any answer prompted further questions and with the nature of our world and the life after death, there comes a point where the answers – if available – must be beyond our comprehension.

In addition to our difficulty in getting our minds round ideas like reincarnation and there being 'no time' in the next dimension, there is my own belief that we should concentrate our attention to the world we are in.

This may sound paradoxical when I endorse rescue work to help lost spirits after mortal death and that work is to help our lives here work better. If we understand how to die better, then we can have less fear and be more comfortable within ourselves. We will also suffer less distraction from lost ghosts who may attempt to possess the unsuspecting, as the numbers of dying people getting lost decreases.

A basic understanding of The Spirit World can help us stay within an honest and harmonic framework for life here, whilst still learning the valuable lessons available through temptation on Earth.

So turning to the questions, with the objective of covering some that may have been prompted with answers where possible and sharing some views on others. Many of the opinions I offer are my own, some were formed from research of channelled works, some through communication directly from Guiding Spirits. In any event the ideas are suggestions and need not be right or wrong. Perhaps many apparently conflicting philosophies can in fact all be right at the same time, there may be no need for mutually exclusive events or beliefs.

What is a ghost?

A ghost is that which remains of a person who has died and is not aware of his own death. The person continues to function as best he can, as if he was still alive. Whilst we could consider a ghost to be a non-physical, non-material energy form the fact that the ghost believes that he has a body may give him some physical form and limitations.

What is a Spirit?

A spirit is the entity or being that we each truly are. Whilst we are in our physical bodies we lose awareness of our true Spiritual identity. Once we die and are aware of that death we can become ourselves again, our Spirit selves. Knowing that spirits do not have physical bodies means that they are truly non-material to the best of our comprehension.

How can we die and not notice?

Death is like a little sleep and we can nod off to death, just as we are only aware of having been asleep when we awaken. There is a close similarity between falling asleep and dying.

How can we tell if we are dead?

Our usual interactions with other people confirm our state of being. If we are ignored and treated as though we do not exist, as if we are invisible, perhaps we are dead and do not exist in the same way as we did when we had a body.

What happens if we die and do not notice?

It seems that when this happens, the ghost wanders around in a state of confusion, often for many years before realising that something is wrong with him. Ghosts seem to believe that other people are ignoring him and blame others rather than accepting responsibility personally and discovering that death has occurred.

Where do these ghosts live?

They occupy the same dimension as we do, but are not in a physical form as we are, therefore we cannot see them. Sometimes people may see them.

When a ghost realises that he's dead, what happens?

They seem to be able then to see other Spirits and are often re-united with their relatives who had died previously. This is a happy reunion in most cases.

What if someone died who has no relatives, who will greet him?

Perhaps an old Spirit friend, someone known to the dead person before their birth. A person who was shown kindness by the dead person may want to welcome him over and show gratitude for the friendly deed.

Is there such a thing as reincarnation?

I believe that there is and I find this most difficult to fit into my head, as I am so focused on the life here and now. I personally believe that we choose to be born and that we accept a certain type of life with a set of challenges or lessons to learn. By being in a body we are able to test our abilities and grow our Spirits. In the disguise of a body, we have the opportunity to deceive others and pretend to be what we are not. As Spirits, I believe all is known and visible, making it harder to devise tests to teach a Spirit to grow. (this big subject could be another book). It seems that after recovering from death, as spirits, we are given a choice about future incarnations. Some choose to come back to learn more while others continue their work on the other side – in the Spirit World.

Who dies aware, and who gets stuck?

The people with fixed and limited ideas and beliefs sometimes get stuck. If you believe that there is no after-life, you will go on believing you are alive whatever happens after your death, as you will think that all awareness must prove that you're alive (not dead). If someone has a rigid idea of what happens on death, they may not believe they are dead until they see what they expect, ie winged angels, St Peter's Pearly Gates etc.

Where do we go after death if we are aware of it?

The description of the after-life from the people who have been classified dead and come back to life, following an accident or medical care, seem to describe the same scene. They talk of a white pearly tunnel made from the light of love and of friends and relatives that come to guide them home to the Spirit World. It seems that we do go to another dimension with our old friends and loved ones.

What do we do in the Spirit World?

After a period of healing and adjustment to acclimatise us for the world where we do not have bodies and other spirits can see who we truly are, we are able to get on with our Spiritual lives. These seem to involve work and recreation. For those who have had bad lives there may be work to do to put right wrongs that were done to others.

What is the spirit world like?

The picture is not clear and hard to describe. I have read many channelled accounts of what it is like in the Spirit World, but fail to really comprehend the descriptions. It sounds a great place with flowers and animals all in perfect bloom and form. A place of harmony and friendship, some descriptions say we still have homes, but I find it hard to understand a world with flowers that is not made of matter.

What sort of work do Spirits do?

I know that some take on the massive task of guiding our lives and they grow through our successes and failures. they present opportunities in front of us and steer us away from unwanted dangers. There may be times when they sit back and let us get into a difficult situation in order that we may learn how to handle ourselves. the work of coordinating our lives and complex interactions must be very demanding.

Do we all have Spirit Guides?

I believe that we each have a group of Spirits who help us get the most value from our lives. Most value, need not mean happiest time, it may be that we have some tough lessons to learn and need a hard life to learn them. It seems that we may have a band of three to five Spirits helping us, also those Spirits may be helping several people at once. They may also be Spirits that we knew as friends before we were born.

Are the Spirit Guides always there?

I think so. Even if they are not they are aware of everything we do, even our thoughts are known to them.

Why say The Lord's Prayer at a seance?

This prayer is well known, not just by us mortals, but by dead people too. Reciting this prayer serves as a statement of an intention to do good and to help others. This brings out the best in the people preparing to attend a seance and reminds them of their purpose. The prayer, when heard by ghosts or playful Spirits, will let them know the purpose of the sitting too; just as a written agenda at a meeting tells people what they are there for.

The prayer for protection, why is that necessary?

The protection prayer recruits the support of respected and loving Spirits who can ensure that the people are not the subject of naughty tricks or are presented with difficulties that may be beyond their ability to solve. It also makes the sitters feel safe; if they feel safe, then they are safe.

How can I prevent myself becoming possessed?

By remaining conscious (not under the extreme influence of drugs or alcohol) you remain aware of yourself, which will enable you to retain control of yourself. If you are particularly receptive or psychic, by remaining conscious you give yourself a greater chance of noticing any outside – ghost or spirit – influences on you. Believing that you are safe and being aware that you have protecting Spirit Guides and becoming conscious of their support increases your safety.

If I believe that I have a ghost hanging around me, what can I do?

Speak to the ghost as though it is there and can hear you and explain that it is dead and invite it to move on. You can even tell it to go somewhere else, but it is kinder to the ghost if you can get it to move to the Spirit World by thinking of its dead relatives or friends.

What are the symptoms of possession?

Acting out of character, having periods of memory loss. Some people develop physical ailments, which are unusual to them and that come and go for no apparent reason. These physical pains are sometimes the pain experienced by the ghost, for example a ghost that died from a head injury may cause a headache when it possesses someone.

Is there a devil?

I don't believe in one. The only person who can harm us is ourselves. After death I understand that there is no judgment, we only judge ourselves. When we are free of our bodies, we can see the wrong we have done to others and we can then attempt to put that right. Imagine if I had murdered someone and then later I'd died. On discovering that there was this marvellous After-Life where all is harmony, peace and love, I imagine that I'd be keen to find the Spirit of the person I'd murdered and apologise and obtain their forgiveness. In this sense there is a Hell equivalent to our own guilt and bad deeds. The worse we are, the more people whose forgiveness we would seek.

Is there a Hell?

Hell is for me, the place described above, where a person dies having wronged so many and so much, that he cannot obtain their forgiveness. Imagine Hitler attempting to get forgiven by all he caused to suffer, or who suffered in his name. Many of those people wouldn't even wait to hear his apology. To me that is Hell, he will have to wait an Eternity to be forgiven by so many. But also those who do not forgive are staying in the memory of suffering and are experiencing a form of Hell themselves. This view is also one that supports Karmic principles, where our's deeds create what we get. We each have the ability to create our own Heaven or Hell. "As ye sow, so shall ye reap". Hence the importance of the message to "do as you would be done by". This is an invitation to accept responsibility for your future and to learn that you create your future – or in modern 'New Age' language *you create your own reality.* So hell is just a state of mind, where one is in the company of their own guilt and unable to deny the truth of their conduct

Is there a God?

I believe that there is a God. What nature that God has I do not know. I find it so hard to conceive the idea of an omnipotent person or being who embodies us all, that I have given up trying to. I have resigned myself to ignorance of God and simply look for evidence of him in all life and in nature. I accept that even if God is just an energy that gives the will to live, then that is ok, but I suspect he is more than that. When I hear people describe the Pearly White Light, I think of that as a vision of love and of God. I am curious but believe God is beyond our comprehension, so I avoid fixed ideas about Him/Her.

Do pets have an after-life?

Yes, I believe they do. There are many channelled examples of Spirits referring to their pets being with them. Even stage mediums see people's pets and use these to identify who, in the audience, a message is for.

Why do some people see ghosts and others do not?

This is only as mysterious as a comparison of any ability or attribute we may possess. Some people, like Pavarotti, Cher, George Michael or Boy George are better singers than others. I think it would be strange if we all possessed the same qualities. Even in supposedly primitive settlements, there would be one Witch-Doctor or Shaman who would be able to predict the future or heal the sick. Not all the villagers would possess the same gifts.

Can Spirits predict the future?

As it seems we are meant to be here to have certain tests and experiences, it would rather defeat the object of the exercise if the future was predetermined. I do believe that certain opportunities and challenges are already mapped out for us to face. These must be known, at some level, to Spirit intelligence. I feel that the Spirits, who are in the know, would understand why it is best that we do not get told the future and therefore would seldom do so.

It follows that future predictions may be offered by Spirits who are not aware of the bigger plan and therefore, I personally doubt the accuracy of such predictions.

We are given a great deal of help and guidance in our lives as we approach new opportunities and I experience this help as a form of intuition. The predictions that I receive are in the form of an internal conviction about the future. Just as I had the conviction that this book was worth working on for several years.

What about past life regression?

Past life regression is a hypnotic technique for getting people to go back in time to previous lives. I feel that this can be of merit if a person is having great difficulty in this life and the difficulty seems unreasonable and may stem from a previous incarnation.

For example if someone has a terrible fear of fire for no apparent reason, no childhood experience seems to have caused it, then it may be discovered, for example, that in a previous life the person was burnt at the stake. With this new understanding the fear can often then be conquered.

As we are unaware of previous lives in our natural state, I personally feel that is how we are supposed to be. If we were meant to recall previous knowledge, we'd be born with it. In view of this opinion, I do not encourage people to regress to past lives very often. I think we are meant to focus on this life and master any difficulties or adapt to them, without cheating and looking up our past.

I have raised this with Spirits and they reassure me by suggesting that if I think I can help someone by using past life regression, then I should do so.

What about suicide?

This is a tough one to answer, as I am conscious of those who read this having lost a friend or relative in this way. It is my belief that when a person takes their own life, they make a huge mistake. Just as all deeds seem to have their consequences and we find there is little we can escape from that we do, so too is the case of using suicide as a way out of difficult life situations.

It seems that for many people who take their lives, they experience their own death and the shock and grief of the person finding their body, over and over again. They discover that it is hard to forgive themselves for the horror they have, albeit in desperation, inflicted on others; sometimes on those who they love most.

The situation they were in, however difficult, was just the lesson they needed to learn from and by suicide, they reject the chance to progress through that lesson. It is my belief that they remain stuck in that situation of their own making until they forgive themselves and they are forgiven for the horror they created through their action.

Whilst this is very upsetting for those who have lost a friend through suicide, it is also an opportunity to clearly forgive that person for their action. This will help them on their path for the sooner we stop grieving the sooner the person is free from their guilt for having left us. Also it is important to me that I express this theory, to help prevent future suicides.

The basic message is, do not take your own life, the consequences are just as bad as the situation you may wish to escape from, so why not just go through the difficulty and learn the lesson that is available to learn.

Why do some people say there is no time in the Spirit World?

The Spirits themselves when they communicate say that they do not have any time in their world. We have time, but they do not. Now I find this hard to understand, but I accept it and really see no reason why time should exist in a world that has flowers, but is not made of matter.

Time is a man made concept and is just a measure of change in one direction. There are channelled ideas that say when we change our present and future, the past also changes. This supports the theory that time need not limit our potential. Some say that the past, present and future all exist at once. That may be how it is possible to make predictions accurately about the future.

Is there any way to prove that there is an After-Life?

I don't believe that proof will be available, although I see a great deal of proof for myself every day. It depends what each of us needs to prove that there is more than this life. Some people see wars and famine as proof that there is no God, for example. Now I see those as a reminder for us to value peace and abundance, it also reminds me that most of the world enjoys harmony.

What I have experienced in the Spirit rescues and communication has been proof for me, but I cannot show anything that would convince a scientific study. I believe in Spirit communication, but I also accept that it is quite valid for a sceptic to suggest that it is simply the expression of the medium's unconscious.

In any event, I think that it's meant to be a mystery so that it serves to develop our faith and trust. There would be less room for temptation and development if everything was already certain. There would be no room for discovery and exploration.

How many ghosts are there?

I'd love to know that answer myself, but I reckon there must be billions of lost souls wandering the earth. After every war I believe some soldiers die in such shock and trauma that they do not know where they are or what is going on and they keep on fighting. I expect there are still Romans marching into battle or defending now ruined sites in their old

Empire. If I find out how many there are, I'll no doubt be shocked by the scale of confusion on the planet. As I feel we are influenced by our environment, until we free these lost souls, they will continue to influence our lives and make us confused.

What is the master plan?

Now if I knew that, who would believe me? Also, I don't believe there are many people who have ever lived capable of comprehending the whole plan. I certainly cannot, but I do think that there is one and we can learn the lessons of that plan by living our lives with truth and harmony. We can learn lessons from all we see around us, be it in the anger of those people we meet, in the beauty of nature or in the death we cause through our greed and pollution.

I don't wish to give lessons on how we should live to fit in with any master plan, as I believe we each decide on our own standards and our own objectives. We create our own lessons and master plan, I recommend we each live to the maximum of our truth.

Twenty-Two

TWO TOUGH ISSUES

Children who die

Even in the most loving world we experience tragedy. Almost as though we need a project to work on to stretch our evolution and trust. The death of a child must be one of the most difficult losses to accept.

Fortunately the experience for the child is apparently better than for those bereaved. From spirit communication it is said that the child 'understands' the separation with its parents and accepts the position due to the broader view that is available once we are free of our bodies.

Some spirits have suggested that the child often stays in the environment of its mother and family and gains the same understanding through development of its spirit that it would have obtained by living the life it has lost.

There have been many bereaved parents who have had the feeling that their child was still with them or even of seeing the child or hearing it playing is common.

In this philosophy, it is important to accept the choice of the child to learn from the new perspective and view this happily so you present the same cheerful environment the child would know and enjoy. It is said elsewhere in this book that our grief and sadness following the death of a loved one, can impede their spiritual progress and growth.

Whilst it is difficult to accept, it is important to be cheerful for the child, after all think of all the difficulties and anxieties it will be free of. No illness, poverty, exams even the stresses of adolescence and the danger of the drug scene are not a danger to that child.

Often it seems that the good die young, and in that respect I consider that once we have learnt our main lesson, which we were born for and accepted as our challenge before birth, we are free to die. If a child is able to be loving, cheerful and generally Mr Happy in the face of a difficult environment or some disability, then perhaps the early death is a sign of passing the test of overcoming that task.

Consider too the freedom gained from any disability or suffering by death. The return to pure love is a better choice and at some mysterious level the person whose life seemed tragically stolen from them may have been resigned by their choice. When we pass exams during our education in this life, if we obtain good grades, we don't retake the exam, we move on quickly to apply what we've learnt and form new objectives. Why shouldn't that include the step from this life to another when the game is won?

For those who you may feel have not passed their test when they die, perhaps they only came hear to provide the test for us. To see how compassionate we really are and then they need suffer no more once we've had our test. Or perhaps they decide to resign from the failure and start again, just as we can tear up a half written letter and start afresh when we recognise our mistakes.

The main point is to be happy for the child, for surely if we believe in any form of loving and forgiving afterlife, then an early death is almost literally heavenly! So be happy for the departed, you'll see them again sooner than you may choose.

The aborted foetus

Even when the child is terminated, for whatever reason be it practical to prevent an unhealthy child suffering a terrible life or for apparently more selfish reasons of bad timing or illegitimacy, the child understands. The spirit of that child, whilst frustrated by the interruption of the chance to be born, can take the wider view and understand the difficulties facing the parents and accepts the situation. The child is sometimes on the waiting list for a different birth and I gather some remain happily in the family and learn from that experience.

With the benefit of the view of love from a spirit perspective there is no bitterness or resentment just compassion and forgiveness, love for the parents who ultimately are spirits limited by the physical world and bodies they are in.

So, if abortion occurs and I'm not judging whether it should or not, accept the unborn spirit as having a deeper understanding than we sometimes credit it with and drop any guilt. That guilt can change nothing and will only create a poor environment should the unborn child decide to stick around to learn its lessons.

If you have guilt that you cannot free yourself from, why not act on it to help others? There is nothing like action to change your difficulties.

Twenty-Three

AFTERWARD

I hope that through reading this book you will have seen that giving up fear of ghosts and death is very healthy. Building a firm belief in a good future and living in accordance with that belief is very a powerful contribution to creating a wonderful life for each one of us.

To know that there is a life after this is motivation for making an effort to be in harmony during this life. This is a belief for motivation from the want of a good future and not as we have tried in the past to motivate good will by fear of Hell and the Devil!

Fear of judgment and Hell have proved partially successful, but in our enlightened times, our so called 'New Age' surely this is the time to take responsibility for the way our lives are and motivate ourselves towards our highest objectives. To aim for our highest picture of the good in each of us.

At least we know now, that if we die, there is something else. We therefore don't need to give up our search for good, to kill others for material gain, when the spiritual future is so much more exciting.

So drop the fear, go for your truth and remember, if you die, keep an open mind. If you find that everyone is ignoring you and you feel invisible – check to see if you're dead. If you find no evidence of being alive, then think of a relative or friend who is already dead and look around for them.

While you're dropping fear from your consciousness, take a last look at grief and let that one go too. It really doesn't help anyone and if we really believe in a life after death, surely we should celebrate our loved one's birthday into a new life! Remember the idea that being really unhappy when someone dies can keep that person so close to us that it becomes difficult for them to move on.

So let go of grief and fear. **Let's get Dead Happy!**

Even if this is all incorrect, and I believe that it's not, consider the benefit of living as though it is. No devil, no powerful organisation that gives out forgiveness. Just you, in charge of your life, getting back what you put out, with the knowledge that one day you'll die and judge yourself. You'll be seeking forgiveness from those you've wronged, you cannot get absolution from sin from some leader of a religious sect, that forgiveness can only be given to you from the God within you after making amends with those that you wronged.

So, I believe we each can take responsibility for our lives and the Heaven or Hell we create. We create our reality totally and will experience exactly the world we believe in. When we die, we will get stuck if we are not open to all possibilities and drop our prejudice and fixed beliefs. There is only truth, love and harmony in all things and it is our challenge to see and experience that truth in all we see and do.

This way of life gives freedom to all people and yet they are their own judge and therefore carry their judge with them, wherever they go. They create it all for themselves.

Good luck, see you on the other side.

Bibliography And Recommended Reading

Therapy & Ghost Therapy
The Unquiet Dead	Dr Edith Fiore
You Have Been Here Before	Dr Edith Fiore
Thirty Years Among The Dead	Carl A Wickland MD
Frogs Into Princes	Bandler & Grindler
Using Your Brain For A Change	Bandler & Grindler
Regression Therapy	Ursula Markham

Near-Death Experience
Life After Death	Neville Randall
Life After Life	Raymond Moody Jr MD
The Light Beyond	Raymond Moody Jr MD
We Don't Die	Martin & Romanowski
Beyond Death's Door	Maurice Rawlings MD
Transformed By The Light	Melvin Morse MD

Channelled Books (or include elements of channelling)
The Nature Of Personal Reality	Jane Roberts
The Return Of Arthur Conan Doyle	Ivan Cooke
The Teachings Of Silver Birch	Edited by A W Austen
Edgar Case On Reincarnation	Edgar Case
Edgar Case The Sleeping Prophet	Jess Stearn

Health & Well-Being
Being Happy	Andrew Matthews
Love Your Disease It's Keeping You Healthy	Dr John Harrison
You Can Heal Your Life	Louise Hay
Creative Visualisation	Shatki Gawain
The Black Butterfly	Richard Moss MD
Love Is The Answer	Gerald Jampolsky
Love Is Letting Go Of Fear	Gerald Jampolsky
Mind To Mind	Betty Shine
The Prophet	Kahlil Gibran

Miscellaneuos
Pendulum Dowsing	Tom Graves
Hungry Ghosts	Joe Fisher
Holy Ghostbuster	J Aelwyn Roberts

Recommended Films

Recommended movies to watch include Ghost, Always, Defending Your Life, Beetlejuice, Ghostbusters, Flatliners, Awakenings, Dead Again, Truly Madly Deeply, My Life.

Recommended Cassette Tapes

Relaxation with Paul – a tape for self-healing and relaxation, available from Ray Brown, 16 Westgarth Gardens, Bury St Edmunds, Suffolk, IP33 3LQ. Price £5 plus £1 for postage and packing (within UK).

Head Cleaner – a Spirit Cleansing/Relaxation Tape by Lance Trendall – for relaxing and cleansing your spirit of any lingering ghosts on side one, with a hypnotic music for your own meditation and relaxation on side two. Available from the author: Lance Trendall, PO Box 69, Harpenden, Herts, AL5 2LY. Price within the UK £7.95 plus £1 post and packing.

There is a form for easy ordering of *Head Cleaner* at the back of this book.

Useful addresses

For Spiritual Healing from Paul, via Ray Brown
Ray Brown, Silver Wings, 16 Westgarth Gardens, Bury St Edmunds, Suffolk IP33 3LQ
Tel: 0284 762599

The Spiritualist Association of Great Britain
33 Belgrave Square, London SW1
Tel: 071 235 3351

The College of Psychic Studies
16 Queensbury Place, London SW7
Tel: 071 589 3292

National Federation of Spiritual Healers
Old Manor Farm Studio, Church Street, Sunbury-on-Thames, Middlesex TW16 6RG
Tel: 0932 783164.

The Greater World Spiritualist Association,
3 Conway Street, Fitzrovia, London W1P 5HA
Tel: 071 436 7555

Lance Trendall
40 Townsend Lane, Harpenden, Herts AL5 2QS

Anglo-American Book Company
Underwood, St.Clears, Carmarthen, Dyfed SA33 4NE
Tel: 0994 230400

The White Eagle Lodge & Publishing Trust
New Lands, Brewells Lane, Liss, Hants GU33 7HY
Tel: 0730 893300
(publishers of "The Return of Arthur Conan Doyle"
White Eagle Lodge promote the teachings of White Eagle and provide a place for free healing, meditation and prayer.)

Rescue Circle (Opening & Closing)

This is an example of a prayer I use in the opening of a rescue circle. The circle is followed by a closing prayer. Before the opening prayer The Lord's Prayer is said by everyone to centre the group.

Opening:

The Lord's Prayer, then:

Dear Friends, thank you for joining us in our small circle as we gather to help others and expand our own consciousness.

We ask that there be help for the sick and starving and comfort and love for the suffering.

As we gather to help those whom you know we can rescue we trust that you will watch over us to guide and protect us.

Amen.

Closing:

Thank you, God bless you and a safe return to spirit.

Keep us safe this night

Secure from all our fears,

May Angels guide us while we sleep

Till morning light appears.

All Is Well

Death is nothing at all

I have only slipped into the next room

I am I, and you are you

Whatever we were to each other, that we are still

Call me by my old familiar name,
speak to me in the easy way which you always used

Put no difference in your tone,
wear no forced air of solemnity or sorrow

Laugh as we always laughed, at the little jokes we enjoyed together

Play, smile, think of me, pray for me

Let my name be ever the household word that it always was

Let it be spoken without effort, without the ghost of a shadow on it

Life means all that it ever meant

It is the same as it ever was; there is absolutely unbroken continuity

What is death but a neglible accident?

Why should I be out of your mind because I am out of your sight?

I am but waiting for you, for an interval,
somewhere very near just around the corner

All is well

Canon Henry Scott Holland (1847-1918)

Twenty-Four

GLOSSARY

After-Life

The spiritual life which occurs after death of the body. The experience after clinical death.

Channel

The path through which energy may flow between the dimensions of the spirit world and the material world, in either direction. A medium may also be called a channel as the medium acts as a channel for spirits to communicate through.

Circle

A seance – a gathering of mortals with the objective to communicate with spirits. This may be a healing circle where the objective is to direct or receive healing energy, a development circle where one may develop one's own psychic abilities. A rescue circle is held to provide a rescue for lost souls or ghosts. Also referred to as 'sitting'.

Clairaudient

To hear psychically, ie hearing beyond the material world, spirit voices. A clairaudient is someone with this ability.

Clairsentience

The ability to sense or perceive something beyond our usual capabilities. Like clairvoyance or clairaudience but without a clear visual or auditory content. A sense of knowing something would fall into this category.

Clairvoyant

To see beyond our material world. This can also be used or someone who perceives the future not necessarily literally seeing. Someone who has this ability can be called a clairvoyant or a psychic.

Dowsing

To use the movement of a pendulum or dowsing rods to determine the position of an object or the answer to a question, in both cases some solution is being sought which is not generally apparent. Water divining – dowsing for underground streams or pipes. Dowsing has been used for the search for minerals.

Entity

A being, often used to describe what is sensed as being there when one feels a person is in the room who cannot be seen. A presence. A being of uncertain nature.

Evil

The ancient concept used to describe an opposite to good. A force still widely believed to be a cause of harm and negative influence.

Exorcism

The removal of a ghost from a place or a body. The halting of a haunting or possession is termed an exorcism. A rescue is the same but it is more of a consideration of the saving of the ghost even though the function is the same.

Ghost

A person whose body is dead who believes he is still alive within a body. This belief is often strong enough for other incarnates to see the ghosts body, hence sightings of ghosts by people who are sensitive to the beliefs of others.

Ghostbusting

An apt term for exorcism popularised by the movie of the same name. A less demonic perception of exorcism.

Guides

The band of spirit helpers assigned to assist each of us. Guardian Angels are commonly believed to exist and these would be spirit guides.

Haunting

The manifestation of ghosts – when witnessed by us mortals is considered a haunting. This can be witnessed by sight of the entity or by evidence of objects being moved, mysterious sounds or just simply sensing a presence. A ghost appearing can still be termed a haunting even if it is not frightening.

Holistic

To look at the whole person, as in Holistic Health Care, the well being of the whole body and whole person is considered. Their emotions and feelings about themselves, what they eat and their general health as well as their physical ailment.

Incarnation

The embodiment of a spirit in our physical form. Hence reincarnation, to once again be born into a physical life.

Inspire

Ideas given to us by some part of us or by spirits. Ideas which seem to influence us but which seem to come from beyond our consciousness.

Manifest

To appear or to show. Ghosts or spirits are often said to manifest, when they are seen by us.

Medium

A person capable of being used as an instrument for spirit communication. This can range from full trance mediumship to clairvoyance and clairaudience. There are many forms of mediumship.

Neuro Linguistic Programming – A science for changing the mental behaviour patterns of an individual by using verbal communication and suggestion to reprogram or change their minds. Established by two psychiatrists Bandler & Grindler who founded a very interesting movement.

Ouija

A board set out with letters of the alphabet and numbers used widely for communicating with spirits who indicate letters in turn by influencing a group of people to move a glass or pointer. Often used by children as a game and this is believed to be a way of communicating with simple and mischievous spirits who are able to operate this very simple form of communication. This method is not recommended by the writer.

Pearly Gates

Biblical metaphor to describe the opening through which our essence or spirit returns to the spirit world. The concept of gates would have been understood by the people of the time. It seems that the pearly gate is really a round (pearl shaped) shaft of bright (pearlescent) light, as described by many who have survived a near death experience.

Pendulum

A weight suspended on a piece of thread able to swing freely to and fro.

Poltergeist

A ghost able to move objects. Often considered dangerous and frightening. Surprisingly these seldom cause harm to people, even though they are often able to move large objects and throw things apparently destructively around rooms. Like some naughty children, they seem to enjoy breaking things and causing disruption, making their presence apparent.

Possession

The act of a ghost taking over a body when done outside of a seance. For example the temporary use of a mediums body for communication during a seance is not considered to be possession. Often a possessing spirit genuinely believes the 'stolen' body to be his own.

Premonition

Foreseeing a future event, which may or may not eventually occur. It is the fact of seeing the vent and not the future occurrence which is the premonition. Often as a result of such a vision new actions can be taken to avoid the event foreseen taking place. The premonition can be a warning to avoid certain things and it can be a feeling and need not necessarily be a visual experience.

Presence

A non mortal entity. A ghost or spirit appearance. To sense a presence you may simply feel that someone is there but be unable to see anyone.

Protection

Safety from mischievous or 'naughty' spirits or confused ghosts. To prevent possession and haunting.

Psychic

One who can utilise senses beyond the five physical senses. A psychic may just know things which are beyond he five senses.

Purgatory

The ancient concept of a place visited after death before going to either heaven or hell. A place of purification through suffering after death, a lost dimension for lost souls.

Reincarnation

To have one's spirit born again into the material world in a new body after death.

Rescue

To enlighten a ghost as to his whereabouts and condition and save him from the confused state where that ghost attempts to communicate with our material world due to his belief that he is still part of it. To allow the ghost to know that he died and enable him to see the spiritual dimension and encourage him to move on into the spirit world.

Rescue Circle/Seance

A gathering of like minded people who meet to rescue ghosts from their confused state of believing that they have bodies and are alive in a physical sense yet do not know where they are.

Seance

A gathering of people to commune with the spirit world. Often to hear from dead relatives.

Sit

To hold or participate in a seance or a circle. A sitting is used to describe a circle or seance.

Soul

The spirit identity of a person.

Spirit

A person who has no body and is alive with the knowledge that he has no physical form or body. He is aware of his presence in the spirit world. This is different from a ghost who cannot recognise his position in the spirit world and remains focused on the material world generally believing that he is alive within a body.

Spirit World

The dimension where people do not have matter or physical space or limitations. The dimension where after-life occurs. The place where spirits go and ghosts have not yet found.

Unconscious

A part of the human mind identified with our actions, which we are not fully aware of. All the functions of the body that occur without our conscious concentration or control, breathing, blushing, heartbeat etc are controlled by this part. Also referred to as the sub-conscious because we are sometimes partly aware of its existence and work. Many of our memories are held accurately in this area, but are not available to our conscious mind as that may confuse and clutter our minds.

Visualisation

To create a mental picture of how something would look or how you would like things to be. A very powerful process for influencing the future or achieving favourable and often exceptional results in the future. Also a valuable technique used in relaxation, meditation and healing.

Head Cleaner Cassette Orders

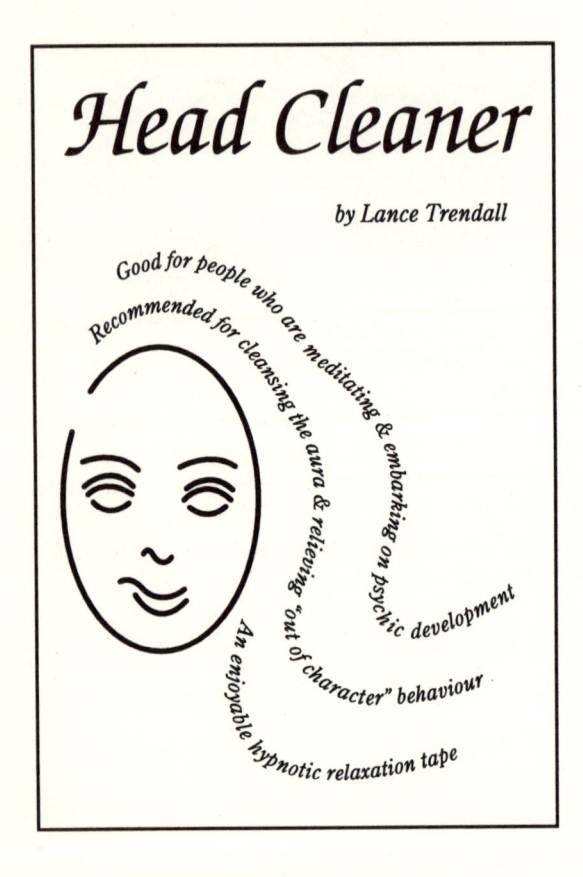

Head Cleaner
by Lance Trendall

Good for people who are meditating & embarking on psychic development

Recommended for cleansing the aura & relieving "out of character" behaviour

An enjoyable hypnotic relaxation tape

SIDE ONE
A guided relaxation to appeal to both your conscious and sub-conscious. Whilst you relax to the words and hypnotic music any "entity" or lost spirit will overhear the words and move to their own dimension safely and with love.

SIDE TWO
The music for your own meditation and relaxation.

To order Head Cleaner by Lance Trendall, please complete the form opposite and send with your cheque/PO for the full amount (£8.95 each) to:

**Lance Trendall
(Head Cleaner Orders)
PO Box 69
Harpenden
Herts AL5 2LY**

Please make cheques payable to 'Lance Trendall'